ADVOCACY

Court Trials ♦ Arbitrations ♦ Administrative Cases ♦ Jury Trials

EXAMINING WITNESSES: DIRECT, CROSS, AND EXPERT EXAMINATION

By

ROGER HAYDOCK

and

JOHN SONSTENG

West's Commitment to the Environment

In 1906, West Publishing Company began recycling materials left over from the production of books. This began a tradition of efficient and responsible use of resources. Today, 100% of our legal bound volumes and more than 75% of our college texts are printed on acid-free, recycled paper consisting of 50% new paper pulp and 50% paper that has undergone a de-inking process. We also use soy-based inks to print many of our books. West recycles nearly 22,650,000 pounds of scrap paper annually—the equivalent of 187,500 tree Since the 1960s, West has devised ways to capture and recycle waste inks, solvents, oils, and vapors created in the printing process. We also recycle plastics of all kinds, wood, glass, corrugated cardboard, and batteries, and have eliminated the use of styrofoam book packaging. We at West are proud of the longevity and the scope of our commitment to the environment.

The cover art, reproduced with the permission of the artist, Hank Virgona, is drawn from a series entitled, *This Honorable Profession.*

Regarding his work, the artist notes:

> "The rule of law is one of the most important pillars of freedom. As an artist who frequently uses satire to make a point, I have always kept in mind the words of Thomas Jefferson: 'the price of freedom is eternal vigilance.'
>
> "My personal observation of the courts has shown that they are only as perfect as those who run them.
>
> "In graphically depicting these observations I have tried, without judgment to show this, for only through honest appraisal can we maintain the vigilance required to safeguard this most vital element of freedom."

Hank Virgona lives and works in New York City.

To: Julie

To: Michael, David, and Molly

*

ACKNOWLEDGMENTS

Many persons contributed to the making of this book. We received substantial support and assistance from our families, friends, and colleagues. We thank them all and greatly appreciate their being a part of our lives.

The students, staff, and faculty at the William Mitchell College of Law deserve special acknowledgment. Renee Anderson, Cheri Fenstermaker, and Cal Bonde greatly assisted in developing this book. Professors Peter Knapp and Ann Juergens provided us with ideas and encouragement. David Herr and other trial lawyers also provided us with suggestions and support. Aaron Dean, Renee Fast, Tiffaney George, Anne Smith, Steve Smith, and Alexandra Schaffer provided research assistance and help.

We also acknowledge those individuals in our earlier book, *Trial: Theories, Tactics, and Techniques*. The Riley v. Garfield House Apartment trial that appears in Book 5 is based on the fact pattern developed by the Association of Trial Lawyers of America. Our publisher and editors at West also deserve our deep appreciation and thanks.

We further acknowledge you who will be reading and using this book. We have written this text for you, for the clients you represent, and the system you serve.

*

PREFACE

ADVOCACY by HAYDOCK and SONSTENG consists of five books:

Book 1—Planning to Win: Effective Preparation.

Book 2—Opening and Closing: How to Present a Case

Book 3—Examining Witnesses: Direct, Cross, and Expert Examinations

Book 4—Evidence, Objections, and Exhibits

Book 5—Jury Trials

These books provide the spectrum of knowledge and skills you need to advocate a case. Each book explains the practice, rules, strategies, tactics, techniques, and theories of preparing and presenting a case. You will learn what to do, where to do it, and why to do it.

These five books explain how to be an effective advocate in all dispute resolution forums including courts, arbitrations, and administrative hearings. The materials present efficient and economical approaches to case preparation and effective approaches to trying cases before judges, jurors, arbitrators, and administrative judges. References in the text to "judges" includes judicial and administrative judges.

This series of books covers civil and criminal trials in the federal and state judicial systems, administrative proceedings, and arbitration hearings. Advocacy by Haydock and Sonsteng is the first publication of its kind to cover comprehensive advocacy skills in all these forums.

What occurs during trials, administrative cases, and arbitrations follow some common and some different rules of procedures. These materials explain both similar and differing practices. Every chapter describes alternative tactics and approaches. There is no single way to plan or present a case. Much of what occurs is determined by the advocate's approach and judgment, and examples illustrated in the text will assist you in making well-reasoned decisions.

The decisions that must be made—from the planning of what to do to the presentation of the case—are based on analytical legal reasoning and incisive judgments. Understanding how to do something and why something is done are keys to a successful case. This integrating process is a primary focus of this series of books.

Advocates make mistakes in every case, and problems commonly occur during cases. The key is not to let the mistakes and problems overwhelm or negate the presentation. Many problems can be anticipated and many mistakes can be eliminated through preparation in an understanding of available solutions described in these materials.

Ethical issues arise during the preparation and presentation of a case. An underlying premise of Advocacy by Haydock and Sonsteng is that lawyers must hold themselves to high ethical standards. An understanding of professional rules and guidelines assist in identifying ethical concerns and resolving problems.

Book One explains how to effectively, efficiently, and economically prepare and plan a case. You will learn how to be a persuasive advocate and how to tell a compelling story. You will learn how to select a case theory and develop a strategy. You will also learn how to choose a forum, select a decision maker, manage a case, anticipate problems, present evidence, identify motions, and act as an advocate. Decisions you may need to make after a case regarding post-trial and post-hearing motions and appeals are explained in case you do win and the other party cannot accept losing.

Book Two describes everything you need to know about conducting highly effective opening presentations and closing summations. Descriptions and examples of organization, structure, storytelling, persuasive approaches, improper approaches, and methods of delivery are provided. Effective ways to prepare and present a motion are also described. Did you think we were going to suggest ineffective ways?

Book Three explains all you need to effectively conduct direct and cross-examination of witnesses, including expert witnesses. The chapter on direct-examination contains strategic explanations and numerous examples of tactics and techniques that will enable you to conduct a persuasive direct examination. The chapter on cross-examination provides a complete explanation of the various types of cross-examination questions and contains numerous illustrations of successful examination approaches, including impeachment. The chapter on expert examinations provides a thorough explanation of alternative topics and questions to ask expert witnesses on direct and cross-examination. Reading this chapter will be more fun than watching Jeopardy.

Book Four comprehensively summarizes and analyzes evidentiary objections and exhibits. Specific procedures applicable to objections are explained in detail, including how to assert and pursue objections and rulings. Explanations and examples of common objections made to direct-examination and cross-examination situations are also presented. A summary compilation of the substantive rules of evidence applicable to court, arbitration, and administrative proceedings is included, including an understandable explanation of hearsay. A comprehensive chapter on exhibits provides specific explanations and examples of foundation questions necessary to introduce a variety of exhibits including common exhibits and modern demonstrative evidence. This chapter also explains the most persuasive ways to use exhibits, in an advocacy setting and at home.

Book Five explains jury selection and jury instructions. You will learn alternative theories of jury selection, how to question prospective jurors, and how to select or challenge potential jurors. You will also learn how to plan and submit jury instructions and all the rules and proceedings governing jury trials. A complete transcript of a jury trial case is included to provide you with an example of an entire jury trial from jury selection to verdict. This transcript permits you to analyze the advocacy theories, tactics, and techniques used by the attorneys, and to second and third guess them.

These books explain the whys and why nots, and the shoulds and should nots of advocacy. The chapters present numerous examples and illustrations of lawyers making presentations and examining witnesses. The examples are based on real and fictional events from the world of history, literature, art, and comedy. We selected events, parties, and witnesses that relate to the topic or skills being explained. Hopefully these illustrations will make interesting, memorable, and entertaining reading.

Our occasional attempts at humor that appear throughout the text may, with the right timing, even be funny. We often take ourselves in practice too seriously, and an occasion guffaw, moan, or snicker may help put things in proper perspective.

We hope that you are experiencing the reality of advocacy practice and its moments of adventure, frustration, excitement, challenge, and enjoyment. We encourage you to send us comments, suggestions, stories, anecdotes, and examples that we can include in our next edition. We wish you the best in being an advocate.

John Sonsteng
Roger Haydock
William Mitchell College of Law
875 Summit Avenue
St. Paul, MN 55105

February 1994

TRIAL PRACTICE TOOLS FROM WEST

Advocacy: Five Books on Essential Skills	Haydock and Sonsteng
The Common Sense Rules of Trial Advocacy	Evans
Bennett's Guide to Jury Selection and Trial Dynamics	Bennett and Hirschhorn
Federal Civil Rules Handbook	Baicker-McKee, Janssen, Berger and Corr
Federal Practice and Procedure	Wright, Miller, Kane, Cooper, Marcus, Graham and Gold
The Trialbook: A Total System for the Preparation and Presentation of a Case	Sonsteng, Haydock and Boyd
Federal Civil Trialbook	Matthews
A Lawyer's Guide to Effective Negotiation and Mediation	Lisnek
Depositions: Procedure, Strategy and Technique	Lisnek and Kaufman
Handbook of Federal Evidence	Graham
Trial Advocacy	Jeans
Effective Client Communication: A Lawyer's Handbook for Interviewing and Counseling	Lisnek
Photographic Evidence	Scott
Federal Jury Practice and Instructions Civil and Criminal	Devitt, Blackmar, Wolff and O'Malley
Federal Court of Appeals Manual	Knibb

Federal Civil Judicial Procedure and Rules

Manual for Complex Litigation

Federal Rules of Evidence for United States Courts and Magistrates

WESTLAW®

Specialized Litigation Databases

AFJ ----------- Almanac of the Federal Judiciary
AMJTA -------- American Journal of Trial Advocacy
BNA–PLD ------ BNA Products Liability Daily
CA–JI ---------- California Jury Instructions
EXPNET -------- ExpertNet®
FSD ---------- Forensic Services Directory
LITIG ---------- Litigation
LRP–JV --------- Jury Verdicts and Settlement Summaries
LTG–TP -------- Litigation—Law Reviews, Texts and Bar Journals
MEDMAL ------- Medical Malpractice Lawsuit Filings
REST–TORT ----- Restatement of the Law—Torts
REVLITIG ------- The Review of Litigation
SCT–PREVIEW --- Preview of U.S. Supreme Court Cases
TASA ---------- Technical Advisory Service for Attorneys
WTH–MDML ---- WESTLAW Topical Highlights—Medical Malpractice
WTH–PL ------- WESTLAW Topical Highlights—Products Liability

Westfax® **West CD–ROM Libraries™** **Disk Products**

WESTLAW
The Ultimate Research System.

To order any of these trial practice tools, call your West Representative or 1–800–328–9352.

NEED A NEW CASE RIGHT NOW?

You can get copies of new court cases faxed to you today—office, courthouse or hotel, anywhere a fax machine is available. Call WEST*fax* at 1–800–562–2329.

June 1994

BOOK THREE EXAMINING WITNESSES: DIRECT, CROSS, AND EXPERT EXAMINATION

TABLE OF CONTENTS

BOOK THREE
EXAMINING WITNESSES: DIRECT, CROSS, AND EXPERT EXAMINATION

ANALYSIS OF SECTIONS

CHAPTER 1. DIRECT EXAMINATION

CHAPTER 2. CROSS–EXAMINATION

*

INTRODUCTION

This book explains how to examine witnesses successfully. Chapter One explains all you need to know and understand about preparing and conducting direct examinations, including numerous examples of effective questions. Chapter Two describes how to prepare for and conduct supportive and discrediting cross-examination and contains numerous illustrations. Chapter Three explains effective direct and cross-examination of experts. These skills enable you to effectively present your case. Do them well, you substantially increase your chances of winning. Do them poorly, and you significantly increase your chances of becoming poorer.

*

CHAPTER 1
DIRECT EXAMINATION

If you can't be direct, why be?

— Lily Tomlin

A. SCOPE

1.01 Why Be Direct?

The purposes of a direct examination are to present evidence:

That is LEGALLY SUFFICIENT to survive a motion to dismiss or a motion for a directed verdict.

That will be easily UNDERSTOOD and readily REMEMBERED by the fact finder.

That will CONVINCE the fact finder of the truth of the story being told.

That will STAND UP to the test of cross-examination.

That will ANTICIPATE, COUNTER, or CONTRADICT evidence submitted by the opposition.

The direct examiner must ask questions that permit the witness to recreate an event so that the fact finder will see, feel, hear, sense, and perceive the event exactly as the witness experienced it. The story told by the witness must be clear, interesting, credible, and convincing. It is the responsibility of the direct examiner to ask questions to develop this story and enable the witness to communicate effectively.

1.02 What is the Evidence?

Four primary evidentiary considerations apply to direct examination:

The witness must be **competent** to testify.

The testimony must be **relevant.**

Foundation questions must establish the reliability of the testimony.

The **form** of the question must be proper.

1.03 Who is Competent?

A witness must satisfy four requirements to be competent to testify:

The witness must give an **oath** or an affirmation to tell the truth.

The witness must have **perceived** something that is relevant.

The witness must be able to **remember** what was perceived.

The witness must be able to **communicate** this information.

The judge or arbitrator determines when a witness meets the requirements of oath, perception, recollection, and communication and is competent to testify. The rules regarding competency reflect practical decisions made by direct examiners. An advocate is not going to have a witness testify who does not understand the oath, does not perceive anything, does not remember, and cannot communicate.

An advocate who plans to conduct a direct examination of a questionable witness may ask for a ruling on the competency of the witness before that witness takes the stand to avoid the opposing party from objecting to a witness. The direct examiner may ask questions of the witness to lay a foundation to establish competency.

1.03.1 Oath or Affirmation

A witness must agree to tell the truth either in response to an oath ("I do") or an affirmation ("I affirm that what I will say will be the truth"). The witness must be able to understand the meaning of an oath or affirmation. Witnesses may be challenged if they are unable to understand what it means to tell the truth, such witnesses include young children or people with mental, learning, memory, or communication disabilities. It may be necessary for the direct examiner to ask a series of questions that demonstrate the witness' ability to understand and tell the truth.

Sample Dialogue

Q: Jeff, how old are you?
A: Seven.
Q: What does it mean to you when someone asks you to tell the truth?
A: It means I shouldn't lie.
Q: What is a lie?
A: It's when I don't tell the truth about something.
Q: What happens to you when you don't tell the truth?
A: I have to go to my room, or I can't do something that I want to do.
Q: Has that happened to you?
A: Yes.
Q: What will you tell us in court today?
A: What really happened to me.
Q: Will it be the truth?
A: Yes.

6.03.2 Perception

The degree to which a witness must perceive something that is relevant depends upon the nature of the testimony. A witness is competent to testify if the witness has personal knowledge of the matters about which the witness is to testify. The rules of evidence exclude testimony concerning matters the witness did not observe or had no opportunity to observe. See Fed.R.Evid. 602. Witnesses acquire personal knowledge through any of their senses.

A lay witness can testify to an opinion if the opinion is rationally based on the perception of the witness and the opinion is helpful to either a clear understanding of the testimony or determination of the fact in issue. Witnesses can testify to opinions within the realm of common experience and which help the fact finder understand an issue. Common lay witness opinions include speed, time, distance, emotions, feelings, age, health, and sobriety, among many others.

A witness may be qualified to testify as an expert witness if the testimony is not generally within the knowledge of the fact finder and the testimony will assist the fact finder in understanding the case or will help establish a fact in issue. Expert testimony includes scientific, technical, or other specialized knowledge outside the scope of the common experiences of the fact finder. A witness is qualified as an expert when the witness has sufficient knowledge, skill, experience, training, or education to render an opinion.

1.03.3 Recollection

A witness must be able to recall what was perceived. A witness whose memory may somehow have been affected between the time of observing an event and trial may be challenged as incompetent. For example, witnesses may be incompetent if they suffered an injury adversely affecting their ability to remember.

1.03.4 Communication

A witness must be able to communicate. Witnesses must be able to narrate what they perceived either through their own words or those of an interpreter. A witness with communication difficulties may be assisted by the direct examiner who may be able to ask leading questions to help the witness testify.

when leading ?'s Ok

1.04 What is Relevant?

Testimony must be relevant before it may be considered by the fact finder. Relevant testimony has a tendency to make more or less probable any facts of consequence to the case. Fed.R.Evid. 401 and 402. If the testimony has probative value, it is admissible. If the testimony has no logical relationship to the case, it is not relevant and therefore not admissible.

While almost all relevant testimony is admissible, there are some exceptions. If the prejudicial value of the evidence unfairly outweighs its probative value, or if the testimony confuses the issues, causes undue delay, or is a needless presentation of cumulative evidence, the evidence will not be permitted even though relevant. Fed.R.Evid. 403. In addition, there are other types of unfairly prejudicial evidence that will not be permitted even if relevant: improper character evidence (Fed.R.Evid. 404 and 405), improper habit evidence (Fed.R.Evid. 406), subsequent remedial measures (Fed.R.Evid. 407), offers of compromise (Fed.R.Evid. 408), payment of medical expenses (Fed.R.Evid. 409), plea bargains (Fed.R.Evid. 410), and liability insurance (Fed.R.Evid. 411).

1.05 What is Foundation?

Evidence based upon unknown or unreliable sources is not admissible. Foundation consists of the facts that establish the reliable source of the evidence. Before evidence of "Y" can be introduced, evidence of "X" must be established. The "X" is the foundation testimony.

Sample Dialogue

Direct Examiner:

Q: What happened when you arrived home?

A: Someone was in the kitchen with Dinah.

Q: Who was it?

Opposing lawyer:

Objection. Lack of foundation.

Judge:

Sustained.

Direct Examiner:

Q: What did you do when you got to the house?

A: I walked into the kitchen.

Q: What did you see?

A: I saw someone in the kitchen with Dinah.

Q: What did you see this person doing?

A: Strummin' on the ol' banjo.

Q: What else was this person doing?

A: He was singing "Fee Fi Fiddley I Oh."

Q: Did you recognize this person?

A: Yes.

Q: How?

A: I had seen and heard him strum his banjo and sing this song at the Grand Ol' Opry.

Q: Who was he?

A: Corky Wharton.

1.06 What is Reliable?

The evidence introduced through direct examination must be assessed to determine its reliability. The following analysis is a method of assessing the admissibility of evidence:

Does the witness have personal knowledge of the matter? Fed.R.Evid. 602.

Has a sufficient foundation been laid to establish the source of the information? Fed.R.Evid. 901–903.

Is the opinion testimony rationally based on the perception of the witness? Fed.R.Evid. 701.

Is the out-of-court statement not defined as hearsay? Fed.R.Evid. 801.

Is the testimony admissible based on an exception to the hearsay rule? Fed.R.Evid. 803 and 804.

If these questions are answered in the affirmative, the evidence is admissible. The following examples illustrate questions establishing reliable testimony:

Description of an Event:

Q: What happened with the harpoon?

A: The harpoon was launched, striking the whale.

Q: What did the whale do?

A: The stricken whale flew forward and dove beneath the sea.

Q: What happened with the harpoon line?

A: With igniting velocity the line ran through the groove until it ran afoul.

Q: What happened after the line ran afoul?

A: Captain Ahab stopped to clear it, but the flying line caught him around the neck.

Q: Then what happened to Captain Ahab?

A: He was shot out of the boat, voicelessly as Turkish mutes bowstring their victim.

Q: What did you see?

A: He was gone. He disappeared into the depths of the sea.

Q: What did you see next?

A: After a while, the whale breached. It shot out of the water.

Q: Did you see Captain Ahab?

A: Yes.

Q: Where was he?

A: He was strapped to the whale, bound by the harpoon lines.

Q: How did he look?

A: Peaceful. His arm was waving at us, beckoning us to follow him.

Q: Did you hear Captain Ahab say anything?

A: Yes.

Q: What did he say?

A: He said, "I spend my last breath on thee."

Description of Sensations:

Q: Shortly before you saw the fire, did you smell anything, Ms. Nero?

A: Yes.

Q: What did you smell?

A: I smelled smoke.

Q: Did you hear anything shortly before you saw the fire?

A: Yes.

Q: What did you hear?

A: A fiddle.

Identification of a Speaker:

Q: Do you know Jan Dean?

A: Yes, I do.

Q: How?

A: I was his friend for years.

Q: Did he talk to you about the accident?

A: Yes, he did.

Q: What did he say?

A: He said, "Gosh, I sure wish that I hadn't gone so fast around Dead Man's Curve."

Description of Opinions:

Q: What did Norma Rae do?

A: I saw her run over to the foreman and shake her fist at him.

Q: How far away from them were you?

A: About three feet.

Q: Did you see how Ms. Rae looked?
A: Yes.
Q: How did she look?
A: She was quite flushed and very excited.
Q: What did she do next?
A: She grabbed a sheet of paper and began writing on it.
Q: How long did you see Ms. Rae?
A: For about a minute.
Q: How would you describe her actions?
A: She was very angry.

Explanation of an Incident:

Q: What did you see, Mr. Frost?
A: Two roads diverged in a yellow wood.
Q: What were you thinking?
A: Sorry I could not travel both and be one traveler.
Q: What happened next?
A: Long I stood.
Q: What did you see as you were standing there?
A: I looked down one as far as I could see.
Q: What did you do?
A: I took the one less traveled by.
Q: Why?
A: Because it made all the difference.

B. HOW TO PREPARE

1.07 The Plan

The preparation of direct examination begins with a review of the legal theories, actual story, and significant issues of the case. Evidence that is necessary to support a theory, fact, or issue needs to be established through direct examination. The direct examination must support the positions taken in final argument.

1.08 The Legal Theories

The elements of each claim or defense must be reviewed to ascertain what direct examination testimony is needed to prove these legal elements.

1.09 The Factual Story

A direct examination must introduce those facts and opinions the witness knows or holds which are part of the factual story of the case. The direct examination of a witness must also establish the foundation for the admissibility of exhibits the witness can identify. Further, the direct examiner must anticipate the cross-examination of the witness and plan to reveal information that reduces the effectiveness of the anticipated cross-examination questions. The direct examiner must also determine whether additional information should be introduced that contradicts or rebuts the opposing side's evidence.

1.10 The Significant Issues

A witness who has information that corroborates important facts, buttresses the credibility of another witness, provides additional information from which the fact finder may draw favorable inferences, or has any other helpful information, should testify to this evidence on direct examination.

1.11 Write the Right Questions

The presentation of an effective direct examination requires the preparation of written materials. These materials may be an outline of topics, a list of questions, or a combination of topics and questions. A written outline provides an organized and structured approach to the examination. The outline includes the major topics about which the witness will testify. The detailed list of questions acts as a script for the direct examination. The materials should be written in large, easy-to-read print, with important words, phrases, and questions highlighted.

A combination outline/script provides the advantages of both while reducing the disadvantages of each. An outline may be effective for easy questions and simple topics, but may be inadequate for complex or difficult foundations or subjects. A detailed script provides a complete list of questions to be asked, but may not permit sufficient flexibility and may encourage the direct examiner to read questions instead of asking questions in a conversational manner. A well-prepared outline/script contains a comprehensive list of topics to be covered and complete specific questions to be asked in certain areas when necessary.

The first step in preparing written materials is to write out all the topics that need to be covered during the direct examination. The second step is to organize the topics by grouping together ones that are related. A third step is to determine their sequence. The next step is to develop questions for those topics. This initial outline/script can be edited and supplemented after the witness has been prepared and after other trial preparations have been completed.

Sample

Background
Name
Address
Family
    Spouse
    Children
Education
    High school
    College
    Degrees
Hobbies

- Job
  - Present
    - Duties
    - Duration
    - Responsibilities
  - Prior
    - Duties
    - Duration
    - Responsibilities
- Day of Accident
  - Date—May 1, 1993
  - Location—999 Westview Drive, Green Acres
- Before accident
  - Where
  - When
  - From—to
- At accident
  - Where standing
  - Lighting
  - Weather conditions
  - Other cars
  - Busy intersection
- Scene
  - Intro diagram: fair and accurate representation
  - NE corner—corner where standing—gas station
  - SE corner—opposite corner—straight ahead—corn field
  - NW corner—corner to left—grocery store
  - SW corner—diagnoal opposite—ball diamond
- Action
  - Blue Chevy going west—right to left on Westview Drive
  - Red Ford going east—left to right on Westview Drive
- Foundation for speed of Chevy
  - How long saw
  - From what distance
  - From where to where
    - Drove car for 20 years
    - Estimated speed of own car and other cars
    - Opinion: 30 mph
- Collision
  - Standing on corner
  - Waiting to cross street
  - Watching traffic
  - Saw collision

Describe collision
Front end of Chevy hit driver's door of Ford
After collision
Ran over to Chevy
Passenger opened car door and got out
How did the passenger appear to you?
Did the passenger say anything to you?
What did the passenger say?
Leave scene
Went home
Contacted by investigator
Conclusion

1.12 Practice and Rehearse

An effective way to prepare a direct examination is to practice asking the questions out loud, following the prepared outline/script. There is no need initially to have a witness provide the answers. Verbalizing the questions familiarizes the attorney with the direct examination, makes the attorney more comfortable with the questions to be asked, and increases the attorney's level of confidence. Changes to the written outline/script can be made during and after this rehearsal. Successive rehearsals allow the attorney to experiment with pacing, timing, voice modulation, gestures, and movement.

C. HOW TO PREPARE THE WITNESS

Witnesses should be prepared and familiar with the testimony they will give. All contact that an advocate has with a witness affects the witness' impression of the advocate and of the case. Factors that may influence the witness' impressions include:

WHO conducts the preparation? Does the witness feel important because the attorney conducts the preparation?

WHEN does preparation occur? Will the witness be more comfortable if the preparation takes place at a time convenient to the witness?

WHERE does the preparation occur? The location, the furniture, and physical layout may affect the impression of the witness.

WHY does the preparation take place? Does the witness understand the role of the witness and the issues in the case to the extent necessary to be an effective witness?

1.13 What Information to Obtain

The gathering of information from witnesses occurs before the initiation of the case and continues through the proceedings. Every contact with the witness should be viewed as an opportunity to prepare the witness. The advocate must determine:

What facts the witness knows,

What opinions the witness has,

What exhibits the witness can identify,

Prior statements the witness has made,

Prior experience as a witness.

What can this witness contribute to the case,

How important is this witness to the case,

What are the strengths and weaknesses of this witness,

What are the abilities of the witness to observe, perceive, remember, and communicate,

How vulnerable is this witness to cross-examination,

Will the fact finders burst into uncontrollable laughter when they hear the witness testify.

1.14 Method Preparation

An advocate must meet with the witness in order to fully and properly prepare that witness for direct examination. The type and extent of preparation varies. Areas to be covered include the legal theories, the factual summary, and significant issues. The more critical the witness is, the more thorough this explanation must be.

Some direct examiners prefer to conduct a mock interrogation and dress rehearsal, complete with questions and answers, of a direct examination and the probable cross-examination, conducted by the attorney or a colleague. Some advocates videotape witnesses so the witnesses can view their answers and their demeanor. Others prefer to prepare a witness by outlining the structure of the examination without rehearsing specific answers to specific questions. The witness may be taken to the room where the proceeding will be held.

Witnesses may be prepared individually, in groups, during one interview, or during several interviews. Some witnesses may have problems that require special consideration before trial. Children, a person with a communication disability, and extremely nervous people, are among witnesses who may need special care during preparation. Specialists, linguists, therapists, or interpreters may assist attorneys with these witnesses. Some witnesses may be rambling, defensive, arrogant, or sarcastic. These problems must be discussed with the witness to reduce or eliminate their negative impact.

The goal of witness preparation is to have the witness testify truthfully and be believed by the fact finder. Some advocates overly prepare a witness by "sandpapering" and "sanitizing" their testimony. All witnesses have some weaknesses and problems. A direct examiner should adjust the approach to each witness depending upon the experience that the witness has in testifying, the importance of the testimony, the witness' ability to testify, and the witness' effectiveness in communicating information.

In addition to personally meeting with a witness, there are other ways information can be provided. The witness can be sent a letter or booklet which explains general information about the proceeding and specific information about the case. If the witness is a client of a direct examining attorney, this written information may be protected by the attorney/client privilege and not be discoverable by the opposing side, except to the extent the information refreshes the recollection of a witness. If the witness is not a client, the written information will most likely be discoverable by the opposing attorney if requested. Another means of witness preparation is the viewing by a witness of a videotape providing general information to the witness about direct and cross-examination.

1.15 Here is the Direct

Witnesses must know what is expected and what will happen. Areas to be covered with a witness include explanations about:

The stages of the proceeding.

The role of the participants.

Objection procedures, including the meaning of the words "overruled" and "sustained."

Practical matters such as transportation, the meaning of a subpoena, the location of the proceeding, when to appear, the place to meet the attorney, the place to wait before testifying, what to do after testifying.

Preparation of diagrams or demonstrative evidence to be drawn on or used by the witness.

Explaining what the attorney may do if the witness forgets something, such as the use of leading questions and other ways to refresh recollection.

The need to testify only to what the witness perceived through the senses of touch, taste, smell, hearing, sight, and what the witness did.

Avoiding speculation, guesses, and assumptions.

Avoiding memorizing answers.

Directions the advocate should give a witness include:

When you are called as a witness, walk confidently to the witness stand and remain standing while taking the oath. Say "I do" clearly so that everyone can hear.

Tell the truth.

Speak clearly and loudly and do not cover your mouth with your hand.

If you will be testifying regarding an event, attempt to recreate in your mind the details of that event. Picture the scene, the persons present, what happened, what was said, and other details.

Listen carefully to the questions and make sure you understand them before answering. If you do not understand, ask me to repeat the question. If you still do not understand the question, say so. Never answer a question you do not fully understand or before you have thought your answer through.

Answer with positive, definite answers. Avoid saying "I think," "I believe," "I'm not real sure," or "In my opinion" when you actually know the facts. If you are uncertain or do not know an answer, say so.

If your answer was incorrect or unclear, correct it. It is appropriate to say "I want to clarify something."

Use your own words and language, not my language or someone else's words.

When testifying, imagine you are having a conversation with the fact finder.

Look at the fact finder when testifying.

Answer the question asked, and do not second guess why I asked the question.

Be aware of body posture.

Dress neatly and appropriately as if the proceeding was a serious, important meeting.

Do not bring any written notes or material to the witness stand unless I tell you to do so.

Immediately stop when there is an objection. Do not try to sneak in an answer.

If there is an objection to the question, listen to the objection and what was said. You may learn something about the question and how it should be answered from these statements.

Be courteous, and avoid disagreeing with me or making jokes.

Do not make gestures or facial expressions which are distracting.

Do not ask the judge for advice. I will assist you.

Anticipate being nervous; it is normal and expected.

If you feel ill, excessively nervous, or fatigued, ask for a break or for a glass of water.

Do not faint or feint when I ask questions.

1.16 Here Comes the Cross

Directions the advocate should give before a witness testifies include:

Answer directly and simply, with a "Yes" or "No," if appropriate. Do not volunteer information or attempt to explain an answer. I may have you explain something on redirect examination if I think it appropriate.

If your answer is complete and truthful, remain quiet. Do not say more even if the cross-examiner looks at you expecting you to say more. If the examiner asks you if that is all you recall, say "Yes" if that is the truth.

Testify to only what you have personally seen, done, said, or heard. Do not speculate, guess, or assume anything. If you do not "know" something because you have not seen, done, said, or heard it, your answer should be, "I don't know."

Testify only to your best recollection. If you do not recall something, do not hesitate to say so, even if you fear this may make you appear to look foolish.

Do not exaggerate, and avoid adjectives and superlatives such as "never" or "always."

Take your time if you need to in answering a question.

If information is contained in a document and you are uncertain of an answer, ask to see the document, or state you do not recall the answer.

If you are asked a question which was asked during a deposition or a prior statement, answer the question if you recall the answer. Otherwise, say you do not recall.

Do not allow the cross-examiner to put words in your mouth. Do not accept the cross-examiner's characterization of time, distances, or events. If a question is inaccurate, state "I cannot answer that question" even if the attorney tries to force you into agreeing or disagreeing with the question or saying yes or no.

If you say something that is inconsistent with your prior testimony, do not collapse. Mistakes will happen. If you make a misstatement, correct it. If you make a mistake, admit it.

Expect the cross-examiner to obtain some information that may weaken your story. Every lawsuit has two sides, and the cross-examiner is attempting to tell the other side of the story.

If the cross-examiner seems confused, do not attempt to help.

Answer trick questions properly:

"Have you talked to anyone about this case?"

You may identify whom you have talked about the case, including the lawyer or other witnesses, or anyone else. It is normal and expected to talk with these individuals.

"Are you being paid to testify in this case?"

You are not being paid to testify. You may be receiving some compensation for the time spent in court away from your work.

"Do you believe the direct examiner has talent?"

Say in response: "The best one I've ever seen in action."

1.17 What To Do

A party or witness who is present throughout the proceeding may need to be advised about certain procedures. They should be told that:

They will be periodically watched by the fact finder and should always be conscious of being observed.

They should periodically maintain eye contact with the fact finder. This helps personalize them.

They should not interrupt the advocate unless necessary or when the attorney seeks advice. It may be preferable to write a note with a question or idea.

They must pay attention and concentrate on the evidence and arguments. They may be able to catch something the advocate missed.

They should not eat in the hearing room, even if Pizza Pit does deliver.

1.18 Whom to Call When

The order in which witnesses testify in a case is a critical aspect of how a case is presented. There are numerous factors that an advocate should consider in determining the most effective sequence of witnesses.

CHRONOLOGY. Witnesses can be called in the order in which the story unfolds.

TOPICAL ORDER. Witnesses may be called in the order in which the attorney presents topics to the fact finder.

FIRST AND LAST IMPRESSION. The witness that provides the best first or last impression about the case should be called first or last.

OVERVIEW WITNESS. A witness who provides a general overview of important events should be called first or early during the case.

PARTY WITNESS. The plaintiff or defendant can be called early during their case in chief to provide the fact finder with the opportunity to see and hear this key witness near the outset.

ADVERSE WITNESS. If a party calls the opposite party as an adverse witness, and if the adverse witness must testify to damaging admissions, this evidence should be presented at a time during the case that presents the best impact.

FOUNDATION WITNESS. A witness who has information needed to establish the foundation for the introduction of other evidence should be called before that evidence is offered.

CRITICAL EXHIBITS. In a case involving important exhibits, it may be necessary to introduce the exhibit at the outset of the case and to call the witnesses necessary to lay the foundation for the introduction of the critical exhibits.

CORROBORATING WITNESSES. A witness who has information which corroborates testimony of a main witness should follow the main witness.

REPETITIVE INFORMATION. If several witnesses will testify to the same facts, it may be effective to separate these witnesses in order to reduce the impression that their stories have been prepared in advance or rehearsed.

WEAK WITNESS. An unimportant witness or an important witness who may have credibility problems or who may be boring should be called when their negative impact is at a minimum.

LAY WITNESSES BEFORE EXPERT WITNESSES. Lay witnesses who establish facts which support the opinion of an expert witness should be called before the expert witness testifies.

AVAILABILITY OF WITNESSES. Some witnesses, particularly expert witnesses, may only be available at predetermined days and times, limiting when they can be scheduled. Their scheduling needs must be accommodated in order for them to appear and testify.

TIME OF DAY/PLACE IN PROCEEDING. The time of the day when witnesses testify and the place they testify in a multi-day proceeding may affect the impression they make on the fact finder. Important or complex evidence may be better received when the fact finder is more alert in the morning or after an afternoon break. The period before or after a lunch or recess may be less productive.

CONCLUDING WITNESS. The last witness in a case should serve one or more purposes, such as: highlighting the case theory, emphasizing important facts, and providing compelling evidence. The concluding witness should not be vulnerable to cross-examination.

REBUTTAL WITNESSES. An important witness should never be saved for rebuttal. If the opposing side chooses not to present the anticipated information needed for the witness to rebut, the witness may not be allowed to testify.

Advocates hold divergent views on which of these factors are the most important. Whatever order of witnesses is selected, the examiner must be prepared to change that sequence. Flexibility may be needed because witnesses may be late or become unavailable on a scheduled day.

D. PRESENTING THE DIRECT

1.19 What To Do

Rules have been established in some jurisdictions that restrict the location and movement during direct examination. Some rules require the examiner stand at a lectern while questioning, and some go so far as to require the examiner stand behind the lectern at all times, permitting the examiner to move only a short distance on either side of the lectern. Other jurisdictions require the examiner remain seated at the table during questioning. Still other jurisdictions provide complete freedom, and the examiner can decide whether it is best to stand, sit, or move about the room.

An advocate who is in a jurisdiction which restricts location and movement may ask permission to ask questions from a different location. Permission should be sought if a tactical advantage exists in conducting the examination in a particular way. Such requests may be summarily denied or readily granted. If asked for a reason, the examiner should explain that the witness will be better able to testify and the fact finder better able to hear or see the evidence if the examination is conducted in a certain way.

The place from which the the direct examination is conducted should be one that permits the fact finder to easily hear the witness and see exhibits and allows the court reporter, if one is present, to hear and see what is said to ensure a complete and accurate record.

In jury trials, some direct examiners prefer to place the jury between the witness and the direct examiner. This placement encourages both the witness and the attorney to speak loud enough so that the jurors can easily hear, focuses the jurors' attention on the witness because the attorney is out of their line of sight when they look at the witness, and encourages the jurors to move their heads periodically back and forth between the witness and the attorney, keeping the jurors more alert.

1.20 How to Approach the Witness

Judges and arbitrators all permit advocates to approach the witness when the examiner needs to show the witness an exhibit. Some require the attorney to ask for permission before approaching a witness. Others do not require the examiner to ask for permission to approach the witness, and assume that if the examiner approaches the witness, it is for a good reason. Those that do require the advocate to ask for permission may only expect the request to be made the first time the advocate approaches the witness.

Sample Dialogue

Direct examiner:

Q: What did you do with the gold medal when you picked it up?

A: I scratched my initials on it.

To the Judge:

May I approach the witness with the exhibit that has been marked for identification as Defendant's Exhibit No. 14?

Judge:

Yes, you may.

1.21 What is Appropriate?

The formal rules of conducting direct examination are limited. However, informal rules and preferences by judges and arbitrators may affect how direct examination proceeds. The advocate needs to be familiar with, or ask about, specific procedures that must or should be followed.

E. HOW TO COMPOSE A DIRECT EXAMINATION

Every direct examination must be organized in a manner that most effectively achieves its purposes. A structure should be selected to enable the witness to tell an interesting, persuasive, and credible story.

1.22 The Beginning

A common and effective way to begin a direct examination is to establish the background of the witness. Background questions accomplish a number of direct examination goals:

THEY RELIEVE some of the initial anxiety of the witness and put the witness at ease. Questions regarding employment, family, and hobbies are usually easy to answer, and help build confidence in the witness. Witnesses will naturally be nervous during the beginning of a direct examination, and simple questions which seek information that is very familiar to the witness reduce this nervousness.

THEY BUILD confidence in the witness to provide longer and more detailed answers. Many witnesses are only able to muster short answers to beginning direct examination questions because of their nervousness. The more questions witnesses answer, the more confidence they gain to provide more information in response to subsequent questions.

THEY HELP establish a witness' personality. Questions which humanize the witness help the fact finder perceive the witness as a person.

THEY DEVELOP the credibility of the witness. Much of the credibility of a witness depends upon the witness' ability to provide answers in their own words which reflect the way they naturally talk. Background questions provide witnesses with an easy opportunity to give responsive answers regarding matters with which they are very familiar.

THEY IDENTIFY similarities between the witness and the fact finder. These similarities strengthen the credibility of a witness because the fact finder may unconsciously or consciously identify with the witness.

THEY ESTABLISH a foundation to support a witness' statement or opinion in the case. In deciding upon background questions to ask, the attorney should review the facts and opinions the witness will proffer and select from the background of the witness information which strengthens the witness' ability to provide the statements and opinions. For example, if a witness testifies to detailed facts, there may be some prior experiences the witness had which affect the ability of the witness to observe or remember detailed facts.

The background of each witness is important, but extensive preliminary information may be much more important for one witness than another. The background of a party or key witness must be developed in more detail than that of a less important witness.

The extent to which background can be developed depends upon the relevance of the testimony to a legal issue in the case, the predisposition of the decision maker to allow a reasonable number of background questions, and the tactical decision by the opposing advocate to object to unnecessary background questions. Many background questions are not legally relevant to a case. For example, whether an eyewitness to an accident has a family or has lived in the community for a long period of time is legally irrelevant to the issues in the case. A reasonable number of background questions are usually allowed, even though the questions are technically irrelevant, as long as they establish the background of the witness. The more important a witness is in a case, the more likely extensive background questions are permitted. The opposing side may object to background questions that are too numerous or go beyond the boundaries of reasonable background information. These objections will be overruled if the direct examiner can establish a link between the background question and an issue in the case.

Some background questions with some witnesses may be more effectively asked at a later stage of the direct examination. For example, the hobbies of a victim of a car crash may have more impact when explained by the witness after the witness has related the injuries suffered which prevent the witness from pursuing these hobbies. Background questions that relate to a specific issue the witness will address should be delayed until the witness testifies regarding such an issue.

Sample Dialogue

. . . *Examination continues*

Q: Then what happened?

A: He came right up to me and demanded all my money.

Q: Did you see his face?

A: Yes.

Q: Do you do anything in your work that helped you remember the man?

A: Yes.

Q: What do you do for a living, Ms. Kay?

A: I am a beauty consultant.

Q: How long have you been doing this?

A: Fifteen years.

Q: What are some of the things that you do on your job?

A: One of the most important things I do is pay attention to the detail of people's faces.

Q: Why?

A: In order to make the correct decisions about what is best for the beauty of my clients.

Q: What have you done to help you with your job?

A: Actually, I study people's faces. Sometimes I am embarrassed because I get caught staring at people.

Q: When you were robbed, what did you do?

A: I stared at the man so I would be able to remember the details of his face.

Q: Describe his facial features.

A: He had brown eyes, brown hair, large cheekbones, a small triangular shaped chin, thin lips, and a bent nose.

1.23 A Structure

Direct examinations must be structured. There are many different effective structures and combinations of structures. The presentation must be simple, clear, easy to understand, informative and persuasive.

1.23.1 Time

The witness can describe the events in the order in which they occurred.

1.23.2 Elements of Claims or Defenses

The witness can testify in the order in which the elements of a claim or defense need to be proved. For example, in civil cases, a witness can first discuss the facts which establish liability and then explain the facts which support damages.

1.23.3 Flashback

The witness can summarize an event and then describe the event in detail. The direct examiner can ask the witness short narrative questions which provide an overview of the entire event and then ask the witness detailed questions which explain the event step by step.

Sample Dialogue

Q: Ms. Daa'e, please briefly tell us what you did at 8:00 p.m. on November 2.

A: I attended a play.

Q: What play?

A: Phantom of the Opera.

Q: What happened after the play?

A: A man came into the box where I was seated.

Q: What did you notice about the man?

A: He was wearing a mask.

Q: Then what happened?

A: He grabbed me and carried me away through a trap door in the stage.

Q: Where did he take you?

A: To the pit.

At this point the direct examiner can have the witness describe the incident in detail.

Q: I want you to tell us what happened step by step that night. What time did the play end?

A: Around 10:00 p.m.

Q: What is the very first thing you saw immediately after the play ended?

A: I saw . . . .

These subsequent specific questions present the details of the incident and are not repetitions of the broad answers.

F. LEADING QUESTIONS

A witness will not be permitted to answer direct examination questions that are phrased improperly. Each question asked on direct examination must be assessed to determine whether its form complies with the rules of evidence. The following analysis provides a method of determining whether questions are proper as to their form.

Does the question suggest the answer? If so, it is a leading question. Fed.R.Evid. 611.

Does the question call for a narrative response? If so, it may be overly broad and improper. Fed.R.Evid. 611.

Is the question repetitious? If so, it may produce cumulative, unnecessary evidence. Fed.R.Evid. 403 and 611.

Is the question vague or ambiguous? If so, it may be confusing or unintelligible. Fed.R.Evid. 401–403.

Is the question a multiple question? If so, it may result in an improper compound answer. Fed.R.Evid. 611.

1.24 Permissible Leading Questions

The general rule that "leading questions are not permitted on direct examination" is a rule of limitation and not an absolute prohibition. The careful use of leading questions within the framework of the rules of evidence may achieve a number of positive results:

They help a witness testify by suggesting familiar topics.

They provide an opportunity to introduce variety into the examination.

They demonstrate honesty by bringing out negative information.

They speed up the presentation of information.

They demonstrate the direct examiner's knowledge of the facts.

A balanced mix of nonleading and appropriate leading questions makes the testimony more interesting, persuasive, and compelling.

Federal Rule of Evidence 611(c) and similar state rules permit leading questions when they are necessary to develop testimony. Rule 611(c) has been interpreted to mean that leading questions are permitted in the following situations:

To bring out preliminary matters.

To elicit non-controversial or undisputed facts.

To establish inconsequential facts.

To suggest new topics.

As transitions.

To bring out negative facts.

To examine an adverse witness.

To question a hostile witness or a witness predisposed against the case.

To lay the foundation for certain exhibits.

To establish complex foundations.

To examine a witness who has difficulty communicating because of age or a disability.

To refresh a witness' recollection.

When asking a witness to contradict a statement made by another.

To lay a foundation for past recollection recorded.

When asking questions during a total eclipse.

Not all of these exceptions are recognized. Many judges and arbitrators do not permit the use of leading questions in all of these situations. The following examples illustrate permissible leading questions recognized by most judges and arbitrators.

1.24.1 Establishing Preliminary Matters—Sample Dialogue

Q: Mr. Dulles, you were Secretary of State in the Eisenhower administration.

A: Of course.

Q: That was a cabinet level position?

A: Yes. I was part of the kitchen cabinet.

Q: What did President Eisenhower like to serve?

A: Spam.

1.24.2 Eliciting Non-controversial or Undisputed Facts—Sample Dialogue

Assume the example below involves a motorcycle accident in which the issue is fault, not the identity of the rider or type of motorcycle.

Q: Mr. Lawson, you were driving Mr. Robert's motorcycle, right?

A: Yes.

Q: It was a V–Max, wasn't it?

A: Yes, it was.

1.24.3 Establishing Inconsequential Facts—Sample Dialogue

Q: You were planning to visit the Great Wall of China, weren't you, Ms. Buck?

A: Yes.

Q: So, much of your conversation was about the trip?

A: Yes.

1.24.4 Suggesting a New Topic—Sample Dialogue

Q: Dr. Ezekiel, what was your occupation?

A: I was the medical examiner for the county of Galilee.

Q: How long were you medical examiner?

A: Fifteen years.

Q: What do you do now?

A: I am retired.

Q: Before you retired you performed an autopsy on the body of Lazarus, didn't you?

A: Yes, I did.

1.24.5 Making a Transition—Sample Dialogue

Q: Private Nord, what did you do on Monday?

A: I destroyed documents in my office using my portable shredder.

Q: Now, on Tuesday you stayed home with your kids?

A: Yes.

Q: What did you do on Wednesday?

A: I again shredded documents in my office.

1.24.6 Bringing Out Negative Information—Sample Dialogue

Q: What did you see?

A: I saw a munchkin run right down the middle of the road.

Q: You don't know who the munchkin was?

A: No, I don't.

Q: Did you see where the munchkin went?

A: Yes.

Q: Where?

A: Straight down the yellow brick road.

Q: Out of sight?

A: Yes.

Q: And you have never seen the munchkin since that day, have you?

A: Never.

1.24.7 Examining an Adverse Witness—Sample Dialogue

Occasionally, the only person who has information necessary to prove a critical element in a case is the opposing party or a person closely identified with the opposing party, such as an employee or agent.

Plaintiff's Advocate:

Your Honor, I call the defendant, Barney Olfield, as an adverse witness.

Judge:

You may.

Plaintiff's Advocate:

Q: Mr. Olfield, you are a famous race car driver, aren't you?

A: Yes, I am.

Q: On April 17, you were driving your car, correct?

A: Yes.

Q: Your car is a 1936 Pierce-Arrow?

A: Yes. It's a beauty.

Q: You drove your car into the back end of plaintiff's car?

A: Yes.

Q: Immediately before the collision, your foot slipped on your gas pedal?

A: Yes.

Q: It was embarrassing for you to have your foot slip?

A: Of course.

Q: So, that is why you told the police the plaintiff had backed her car into yours at a speed of 25 miles per hour?

A: I'm afraid so.

1.24.8 Questioning a Hostile Witness—Sample Dialogue

An independent witness who demonstrates a reluctance to testify or hostility becomes a hostile witness and may be cross-examined.

Direct Examiner:

Your Honor, this witness is a hostile witness. She is angry with the police and my office for prosecuting her friend. While she initially said she would not talk about how much the defendant had to drink, she is now willing to do so but with much reluctance. I am uncertain what she will say. I request the opportunity to use leading questions during the direct examination under the provisions of Rule 611(c).

Judge:

You may do so.

Direct Examiner:

Q: Are you the defendant's friend?

A: Yes.

Q: You are angry with the police for arresting him for drunk driving?

A: That's very true.

Q: Do you want to help the defendant?

A: Yes.

Q: You don't want to be here to testify for the prosecution, do you?

A: No.

Q: You told the police that you did not want him to go to jail, and that you would not tell anybody about how much you saw him drink?

A: Yes.

Q: It is true that you saw the defendant drink an entire bottle of wine and then drive his car?

A: Yes, that's true, but it was a 1968 French Bordeaux that had fine clarity.

1.24.9 Laying Foundation For Exhibits—Sample Dialogue

Q: Mr. Noah, I have just handed you a photograph which has been marked for identification as Plaintiff's Exhibit No. 2. Do you recognize it?

A: Yes, I do.

Q: What is it?

A: It is a picture of our Ark.

Q: How do you know?

A: Well, it looks just like we left it when we beached it on Mount Ararat.

Q: Is Plaintiff's Exhibit No. 2, marked for identification, a fair and accurate representation of how your Ark looked the day before the flood?

A: Yes.

1.24.10 Establishing a Complex Foundation—Sample Dialogue

Q: As a laboratory analyst, Ms. Curie, based on your education, training, experience, and the testing of this substance, do you have an opinion to a reasonable degree of scientific certainty what this substance is?

A: Yes.

Q: What is your opinion?

A: It is law school vending machine food.

1.24.11 Examining a Witness Who Has a Difficult Time Communicating—Sample Dialogue

Q: How old are you, Gretel?

A: Four.

Q: Do you remember what happened to your brother, Hansel?

A: Yes.

Q: He's not here anymore, is he?

A: No.

Q: Do you know what happened to him?

A: Yes.

Q: What happened?

A: We were playing in the woods.

Q: What did you see in the woods?

A: A house.

Q: Did you go into the house?

A: Yeah.

Q: What happened?

A: I saw an elderly woman put Hansel in the oven.

1.24.12 Asking a Witness to Contradict a Statement Made by Another—Sample Dialogue

Q: Mr. Sanford you heard your son testify that the noisy argument took place out in the street, didn't you?

A: Yes, I heard that.
Q: Is that what you recall about the argument?
A: No, it isn't.
Q: Where did the argument take place?
A: The argument occurred in the back alley.

G. ADDITIONAL QUESTIONS

1.25 Refreshing a Witness' Recollection

A witness may have a memory lapse. A previous statement or some other evidence may be provided to help the witness recall the answer. Sometimes it is sufficient to ask one or two quick leading questions to jog a witness' memory.

The direct examiner may also show a document to the witness to refresh the witness' memory. The examining attorney must first establish that the witness now has no memory of the answer about which the witness is being questioned. The witness may review the statement and then must set it aside before answering, since the answer must not be from the document itself, but must be from actual refreshed memory.

The witness should not read from the statement for two reasons. First, it is improper and objectionable. If the witness reads a prior statement, that statement is actually being introduced as past recollection recorded. Federal Rule of Evidence 803(5) requires a specific foundation for the introduction of a document as a previously recorded recollection. In practice, the difference between refreshing recollection and past recollection recorded is often ignored and witnesses are frequently permitted to review their notes or statements while testifying. Second, if the witness reads from a statement or document, the witness becomes vulnerable to cross-examination questions which highlight that the witness has no independent recollection of what occurred and may not be believable.

Documents used to refresh recollection do not usually need to be marked as an exhibit. The refreshing items are often not marked because they are not offered as evidence. The only evidence is the oral testimony of the witness. The cross-examiner has a right to see the written statement or document or item used to refresh, and can use it during cross-examination. See Fed.R.Evid. 612. The opposing advocate may have the document marked and introduce it into evidence for impeachment or as an admission.

In some situations witnesses may bring notes with them to help refresh recollection. Police officers, administrators, and some experts often bring a file with them to the witness stand and use it to refresh their memory during testimony. The opposing advocate may insist that the notes be used properly. That is, the advocate may either ask that the witness put the notes away and testify independently without reference to the notes or have the direct examiner lay the proper foundation.

Sample Dialogue

Q: Mr. Chase, when you loaded up the car for your vacation, what did you pack?

A: Picnic gear, raincoats, regular clothes, suitcases, Wally World map, Aunt Edna . . . Let's see, I think that's it.

Q: Do you remember putting anything else in the trunk?

A: That's all I can remember.

Q: Did you pack five sets of scuba gear and five pairs of snow skis?

A: How silly of me, of course.

Q: Mr. Chase, do you remember putting anything else in the trunk?

A: That's all I can remember. There may have been more.

Q: Is there anything that would help refresh your recollection as to what else you might have put in the trunk?

A: Yes, my letter to the insurance company. I listed everything that was stolen.

Q: I have just given you a letter. Do you recognize it?

A: Yes, it is my letter to the insurance company.

Q: Read it please.

A: All right.

Q: Does reading that letter refresh your recollection as to what else you put in your trunk?

A: Yes.

Q: May I have it back, please?

A: Yes, here is the letter.

Q: Do you now remember what else you put in the trunk?

A: Yes.

Q: What?

A: Five sets of scuba equipment and five pairs of snow skis.

1.26 Narrative Questions

A narrative question may be proper or improper, depending upon the scope of the question, the timing of the question, the ability of the witness to answer, and the ability of the direct examiner to control the witness. A narrative question is improper if:

The witness responds with a long, uncontrolled story, or

The narrative response denies the opposing attorney the opportunity to anticipate objectionable evidence and the ability to make a timely objection, or

The narrative question reduces the ability of the direct examiner to control the direction or the scope of the examination.

Judges and arbitrators have broad discretion in permitting or limiting the use of narrative questions by determining the capabilities of the witness to properly testify and the capabilities of the direct examiner to control the examination. A judge or arbitrator is likely to permit narrative questions asked by an effective direct examiner, and is likely to permit narrative responses by a properly prepared witness who can appropriately respond to a question.

Specific forms of narrative questions are commonly asked during direct examinations. Narrative questions that are limited in scope or that act as transition questions are usually appropriate, such as "What happened next?" or "Then what happened?" The timing of the narrative question may also influence its propriety. A broad, narrative question asked at the beginning of a direct examination may more likely not be permitted because the capabilities of the witness have not been established. Narrative questions asked later during the examination of a witness are more likely to be permitted to assist the witness to continue describing a story in sequence.

Sample Dialogue

Q: Mr. President, what happened in the voting booth on the second Tuesday in November?

A: I voted for Alfred E. Neuman.

Q: Then what happened?

A: I lost the election.

1.27 Vague or Ambiguous Questions

All questions must be reasonably clear and specific so that the witness knows what is being asked, the other side knows whether to object and the fact finder can understand the testimony. Vague, ambiguous, confusing, unintelligible, and misleading questions must be avoided.

Sample Dialogue

Q: Did you, subsequent to your conversation with the investigator, affix your signature to a testimonial document?

A: What?

Q: Let me rephrase the question. Did you sign the piece of paper that Mr. Magnum gave you?

A: Oh! Yes, I signed it.

1.28 Repetitious Questions

A witness is generally permitted to describe what happened only once. An unfair advantage may not be gained by repeating favorable testimony over and over again. The form of the question need not be identical to be repetitious. Questions may be asked during direct examination to clarify prior responses, add descriptive details to a story, and emphasize testimony. The key is to avoid asking questions that sound repetitive or produce answers which are repetitive.

Sample Dialogue

Q: What happened next Ms. Rashad?

A: I held on to the strap of the briefcase, and he had hold of the other end and was pulling it away from me. I tried to pull it away from him, and then he yanked real hard and pulled it out of my grasp.

Q: How did you try to pull it away from him?

A: I had the newspaper in my left hand, and I gripped the strap with my right hand, and pulled my arm towards my body.

Q: How did he yank the briefcase away from you?

A: He grabbed on to the bottom of the briefcase with both hands and pulled it right out of my hands.

Q: How did he grab on to the briefcase?

A: With both hands.

1.29 Multiple Questions

Multiple or compound questions are impossible to understand and create a jumbled court record. It is often unclear what part of the multiple question the witness answered. Compound questions should be withdrawn and rephrased.

Sample Dialogue

Q: When did you wake up, and what did you see when you awoke? Excuse me. I'll withdraw the question and rephrase it. What day did you wake up, Mr. Van Winkle?

H. HOW TO ENHANCE PERSUASIVENESS

This section presents a variety of questioning techniques that can be employed to conduct an effective direct examination.

1.30 Use Background Questions

These preliminary questions have nothing to do with the case specifically. Questions can be asked to help put the witness at ease as well as establish that the witness is competent.

Sample Dialogue

Q: Jimmy, is your last name Olson?

A: Yes.

Q: How old are you, Jimmy?

A: I am going to be eight.

Q: When are you going to be eight?

A: When my birthday comes.

Q: Do you have any brothers or sisters?

A: Marni and Marci.

Q: What do you like to do most of all?

A: Play with my computer.

Q: What is your favorite computer program?

A: Superman.

1.31 Establish a Witness' Personality

The background of the witness is necessary to establish a personality and the credibility of the witness.

Sample Dialogue

Q: Tell us your name please.

A: Vanna Gray.

Q: Ms. Gray, what is your occupation?

A: I am a hostess for a television game show.

Q: What does that involve?

A: All that I am really required to do is to dress fashionably and to turn letters on a big board as contestants guess them.

Q: Is that it?

A: Yes, it is.

Q: Do you have to do much talking on the show?

A: No.

Q: How did you get into that business?

A: When I finished college, I moved to California and for the fun of it, I auditioned for the job and got it.

Q: When did you move to California?

A: About ten years ago.

Q: Where did you go to college?

A: The University of Linguistics.

Q: What did you get your degree in?

A: I received a degree in etymology.

1.32 Demonstrate Credibility

The experiences of a witness help establish the credibility of that witness. Information which establishes a connection between the experiences of a witness and the evidence should be established.

Sample Dialogue

Q: Mr. Chan, were you requested to investigate an automobile accident in which Ms. Miyamoto was involved?

A: Yes, I was.

Q: What did you do to investigate this accident?

A: I went out to the accident site and saw Ms. Miyamoto's black Stingray and the other car. I photographed the scene from many different vantage points and photographed the vehicles as they were parked in a parking lot near the intersection. I noticed the skidmarks on the street, measured their length and photographed them. I also took close-up photographs of all the damaged parts of both vehicles. I wrote up fact sheets on all of my observations and attached the developed pictures to each of the appropriate fact sheets.

Q: Describe the training that you have had in photography and particularly in taking pictures of accident scenes?

A: I worked as a member of a highway patrol crime and accident scene team for twenty-five years until my retirement three years ago. In the last three years, I have had my own business, Cannon Ball Investigative Services. I have taken forty hours of training in photography through Kodak company and I have studied photography at the University.

Q: Can you estimate how many accident scenes you have investigated and photographed over the last twenty-eight years?

A: Yes.

Q: How are you able to do that?

A: When I started my business, I knew it would be important to be able to provide that information in order to show my experience in the field if I was called upon to testify in court. I went back to the department and went over all of my reports through the use of the computer and was able to determine how many accidents I had investigated. Since I started my own business, I have kept careful records.

Q: How many accident scenes have you investigated and photographed over the last twenty-eight years?

A: Very close to 4,000.

1.33 Display the Sincerity of the Witness

When witnesses are given the opportunity to talk about their lives, jobs, friends, and acquaintances, in their own words, they demonstrate they are honest and sincere persons. This will enhance the effectiveness of their testimony concerning the case.

Sample Dialogue

Q: Mr. Clyde, as a bank robber, what kinds of things do you have to do?

A: I have to plan every robbery, buy the bullets, keep track of the money, and be able to shoot accurately.

Q: What details do you plan?

A: We must plan each robbery with great detail. We must know how many persons are working in each bank and how many guards are on duty. We must determine how long we can be in each bank before the police show up; and, of course, we have to know when the payroll arrives at the bank.

Q: How often do you rob banks?

A: Quite regularly. In the winter we head south. In the summer we head north.

Q: Do you take any breaks between bank robberies?

A: Yes.

Q: How do you take these breaks?

A: Well, every robbery is a little bit different, and so are the breaks. We usually take a week break between banks, sometimes longer, if we get chased.

Q: Are these breaks important?

A: Yes.

Q: Why?

A: Well, there is some strain in robbing banks and to relieve tension and make sure that we don't make mistakes, me and Bonnie and the gang take regular breaks to relax and to help us keep our skills sharp.

1.34 Identify Similarities Between the Witness and the Fact Finder

Answers may establish similarities between a witness and the fact finder.

Sample Dialogue

Q: Tell us your name?

A: Mr. Spock.

Q: Where do you live?

A: Live?

Q: Yes, where are you from?

A: I see. I am from the Planet Vulcan and that is where I make my home when I am not working.

Q: Where do you work?

A: I am assigned to the Star Ship Enterprise.

Q: And where is the Enterprise now?

A: In the Milky Way—coordinates starpoint 4896.12.

Q: What is your assignment on the Enterprise?

A: I am the first officer.

Q: Do you have any time for hobbies?

A: Yes, I do.

Q: Tell us please what your hobbies are.

A: Well, I do like to travel. I enjoy camping. One of my favorite places is Yosemite. I like sports, particularly bowling. I enjoy reading, especially twenty-first century history.

I. HOW TO LAY A FOUNDATION

1.35 Establish Perception

Facts must be established to show that the witnesses saw or heard what they say they saw or heard.

Sample Dialogue

Q: What happened next?

A: I saw this man walk up to my ticket window and stand right in front of me.

Q: What were the lighting conditions like at that time?

A: There were bright lights on both sides of the ticket window, and there was a light on in the ticket window.

Q: Describe the ticket window you were looking through when you saw the man standing in front of you.

A: It's a clear plate glass window, about 2 feet wide and 3 feet high with a 6 inch opening to pass money and tickets.

Q: What condition was it in on that day?

A: It was clean, and there was nothing blocking my view.

Q: Describe the man you saw, Ms. Ortega?

1.36 Enhance Foundation

Foundation questions should be asked that enhance the reliability and accuracy of the story told by the witness.

Sample Dialogues

Q: Mr. Fife, where were you at three o'clock p.m. on April 2, two years ago?

A: I was at the northeast corner of the intersection of Lexington and Grand Avenues in our city.

Q: What were you doing?

A: I was working as a crossing guard, watching traffic.

Q: What did you see?

A: I saw a collision between a red Honda and a blue BMW.

Additional foundation questions further enhance the reliability and accuracy of the witness' story.

Q: What is your educational background, Mr. Fife?

A: I have a degree from Mayberry High School.

Q: How long ago?

A: Thirty-three years.

Q: Since you graduated from high school, what further education have you had?

A: Courses that helped me in my career like driving school, traffic training, weapons training, not with real bullets, of course, and other police courses needed to sharpen my keen law enforcement skills.

Q: Since graduation what has been your work experience in the field?

A: Well, I haven't worked a lot in the field but I have worked here in town for twenty-five years as a deputy for Sheriff Andy Taylor.

Q: Have you had any special titles?

A: Yes, I am the Guard in Charge of the Mayberry Elementary School crossing.

Q: What are your responsibilities?

A: It is my duty to make sure that all the children get across the street safely, and that means that I have to watch the cars and the children very carefully.

Q: Have you had any special training for this assignment?

A: Yes.

Q: What?

A: Well, Sheriff Taylor sent me to traffic training where I learned the most modern methods of school crossing techniques. And then during the day when the kids are in school, I go out and practice at the crossing, making cars stop and go.

Q: Please describe to us what you saw at the intersection of Lexington and Grand Avenues at three o'clock p.m. on April 2, 1992.

1.37 Establish Foundation to Support an Opinion

Before a witness can render an opinion, questions need to be asked which show that the witness perceived events which support the opinion or conclusion.

Sample Dialogue

Q: Were you in the room when John Greystoke signed the will?

A: I most certainly was.

Q: Did you see what he was doing before he signed the will?

A: Yes, I did.

Q: What was he doing?

A: He was swinging from the chandelier, chattering like a baboon.

Q: How long had you know Mr. Greystoke?

A: Twenty years.

Q: How often had you seen him?

A: Weekly over that time.

Q: Had you ever seen him swing from the chandelier before?

A: Only a few times.

Q: How did he sign the will?

A: He first tried to squash his banana on it.

Q: Then what?

A: His butler gave him a pen and he made a "T" on the will.

Q: Do you have an opinion if Mr. Greystoke knew what he was doing when he signed the will?

A: Yes.

Q: What is that opinion?

A: He had no idea what he was doing.

1.38 Set the Scene

Most stories, plays, motion pictures or re-creations of actual events must be placed in a setting that the audience can visualize. The same is true with a direct examination. The scene must usually be established before the action can make sense. Once that scene has been established by primary witnesses, later witnesses may be placed at the scene to confirm the accuracy of what has been established and then to describe the action from their perspective. As the action shifts to a new location, the scene must be set again by witnesses.

It is important for the direct examiner to focus the witness and the fact finder on the perspective from which the examiner wants them to see the scene. The scene may be described from two perspectives: through the eyes of the witness or from an overview. The first has the witness act as a storyteller and use phrases "I saw" and "I could see." The second has the witness act like a historian and describe a scene.

(A) Establishing the View of the Witness

In this example the fact finder sees the scene from the viewpoint of the witness.

Sample Dialogue

Q: As you were walking down the driveway, what did you see directly in front of you?

A: I saw large, old oak trees and magnolia trees lining both sides of the path.

Q: What did you see directly to your right?

A: I could see a large home with white columns and ivy growing on the brick walls.

Q: What did you see as you looked to your left, Ms. O'Hara?

A: I saw the burned-out shell of the house that was destroyed by the explosion and fire.

(B) Establishing an Overview

Although some fact finders may place themselves at eye level with the witness, others may be looking at the scene from above or from some other vantage point. If a diagram is used, it may place the fact finder above the scene.

Sample Dialogue

Q: What kind of driveway was it?

A: Cobblestone.

Q: Was there anything on either side?

A: Yes.

Q: What?

A: Old oak trees and magnolia trees ran the length of the path on either side.

Q: What is on the right side of the driveway near the entrance?

A: A large house with white columns and ivy growing on the brick.

Q: What is on the left?

A: The burned-out shell of the house that had been destroyed by the Yankees.

1.39 Describe Details

The fact finders should be told every detail necessary to accurately understand the scene as the attorney wants them to understand it to satisfy their reasonable curiosity. Unnecessary details should be left out since excessively precise descriptions may be boring and a waste of time.

Sample Dialogue

Q: What kind of neighborhood was it, Mr. Matzeliger?

A: It was an older neighborhood, with large homes and one newer building that contained apartments for adults only. There was a shoe store on the corner.

1.40 Describe the Action

It is most appropriate for a witness to describe events as they happened. The direct examiner should ask questions in a structured way so that it is easy for the witness to explain events to enable the fact finders to understand and be able to clearly visualize what happened. A chronological order is usually easy to follow. Good literature is filled with captivating descriptions of people, places, and action.

1.41 Describe a Person—Sample Dialogue

Q: After you came downstairs and went into the living room, what did you see?

A: I saw a man standing by the fireplace.

Q: How were you able to see him?

A: The table light and the Christmas tree lights were on.

Q: What was he wearing?

A: A red outfit.

Q: Please be more specific.

A: He was dressed in fur, from his head to his foot.

Q: Were his clothes clean or dirty?

A: They were all tarnished with ashes and soot.

Q: Describe his general build for us?

A: He was chubby and plump.

Q: What did his face look like?

A: His eyes twinkled. He had dimples and appeared merry.

Q: Go on?

A: His cheeks were like roses, his nose like a cherry.

Q: What was his mcuth like?

A: He had a droll little mouth which was drawn up like a bow, and he had a beard on his chin that was as white as the snow.

Q: Did he have anything in his mouth?

A: Yes.

Q: What?

A: Well, he had a stump of a pipe which he held tight in his teeth.

Q: Was he carrying anything?

A: Yes.

Q: What?

A: He had a bundle of toys which he had flung on his back.

Q: What did he look like?

A: He looked like a peddler just opening his pack.

Q: What else can you remember about this man?

A: He had a broad face and a round little belly that shook when he laughed, like a bowl full of jelly.

Q: Is there anything else that he did besides laugh?

A: Yes, he winked at me and twisted his head.

Q: What did you feel when he did that?

A: I felt that I had nothing to dread.

1.42 Describe an Event—Sample Dialogue

Q: What is your name please?

A: Officer Alonzo Mosley.

Q: Where do you work?

A: For the City of Hastings.

Q: What do you do for the City?

A: I am a police officer.

Q: How long have you been a police officer?

A: Ten years.

Q: Were you working on May 1st this year?

A: Yes.

Q: At 11:00 p.m. on May 1st this year were you on duty?

A: Yes, I was.

Q: Where were you at 11:00 p.m.?

A: I was at the intersection of 71st Street and Newton Avenue.

Q: Were you on foot or in a car?

A: In a police car.

Q: What did you see?

A: I saw a bright red Chrysler roadster.
Q: Which way was it traveling?
A: North to south on Newton Avenue.
Q: What did you see about the car?
A: It was traveling on the wrong side of the road and appeared to be traveling very fast.
Q: What did you do?
A: I began to follow the car.
Q: What was the car doing?
A: It was weaving wildly from side to side of the entire road. Twice it drove up on the curb and bounced back down on the road.
Q: Was your car equipped with radar?
A: No, it was not.
Q: Were you able to determine how fast the car was traveling?
A: Approximately.
Q: How?
A: I sped up and got behind the car. At that time, I was able to match my speed with the car for about one block. I stayed about 150 feet behind the car because of its weaving from side to side. My speedometer indicated that my car was traveling 40 miles per hour.
Q: Do you know what the posted speed limit is on Newton Avenue where you were?
A: Yes, I do.
Q: What is it?
A: Thirty miles per hour.
Q: What did you do?
A: I followed the red Chrysler for about two blocks and then I turned on my overhead red lights and siren.
Q: What happened?
A: The car kept on going on the wrong side of the street for another block and then it finally stopped on the wrong side of the street.
Q: What did you do?

A: I shined my spotlight on the car and walked up to the driver's side.

Q: What did you see when you approached the car?

A: I saw a man in his early sixties sitting behind the wheel. He was wearing a white suit, no tie.

Q: What else did you notice?

A: When the man rolled down the window of his car, I could smell a strong odor of what I believed to be alcohol coming from inside the car.

Q: What did you do next?

A: I asked him to get out of the car and he did. I asked if he had a driver's license.

Q: Did he give you a license?

A: No.

Q: Did he say anything to you?

A: Yes, he did.

Q: What?

A: He said that he did not have a license, had never had one, and didn't need one.

Q: How did he speak?

A: His speech was very slurred. I could hardly understand what he said.

Q: Could you see his face clearly?

A: Yes.

Q: How?

A: I had my flashlight shining near his face, the police car spotlight shined on us, and we were standing directly under a street light.

Q: Describe his face for us.

A: His face was flushed and reddish. He appeared to be sweating, and his eyes were bloodshot, glassy, and watery.

Q: Could you smell his breath at that time?

A: Yes.

Q: How close were you when you could smell his breath?

A: About two feet.

Q: What could you smell?

A: I could smell the strong odor of an alcoholic beverage.

Q: What did you do next?

A: I asked him to take what are called "Field Sobriety Tests."

Q: Why do you ask a person to take field sobriety tests?

A: To determine the ability of a person to coordinate movements, retain balance, follow simple directions and perform simple tasks.

Q: What is the first test that you asked him to perform?

A: I asked him to stand erect with his feet together and his arms outstretched. I told him to close his eyes and touch the tip of his nose with first his right index finger and then with his left.

Q: How did he do when he tried to touch his nose with his right hand?

A: First he started to fall over and I caught him and stood him up. However, he did not open his eyes. He then touched the middle of his forehead with his index finger and slid it down along his nose to the tip.

Q: How did he perform with his left hand?

A: He touched the side of his upper lip and slid his finger up to his nose.

Q: Did you ask him to perform another test?

A: Yes, I did.

Q: What?

A: I asked him to say the alphabet.

Q: How did he do?

A: He did fine until he got to the letter "K" and he then said "K" eight or nine times and finally said, "I can't remember any more."

Q: Did you ask him to take any more tests?

A: Yes.

Q: What test?

A: I asked him to walk a straight line, one foot in front of the other.

Q: Did he take that test?

A: No.

Q: Did he tell you why?

A: Yes.

Q: What did he say?

A: He said, "I ain't takin' any more tests. I'm as drunk as an old skunk. You've got me now and you know it."

Q: What did you do then?

A: I placed him under arrest for driving while under the influence of an alcoholic beverage. I then drove him to the county jail and offered him a breath test.

Q: What happened when you offered him a breath test?

A: He refused to take a breath test. I then offered him a chance to provide a urine or blood sample.

Q: Did he give you any samples?

A: No.

Q: What did you do then?

A: I left him at the jail with the county sheriff and went back on patrol.

Q: Did he ever tell you his name?

A: Yes, he said his name was Bacchus.

Q: Just Bacchus?

A: That's right. He said that was the only name he had.

Q: In the years on the police force have you arrested people for driving under the influence of alcohol?

A: Yes, hundreds of times.

Q: Do you ever drink alcoholic beverages?

A: Yes, I do, on occasion.

Q: Have you seen other people drink?

A: Yes.

Q: Have you seen some of these people come under the influence of alcohol?

A: Yes, I have.

Q: Based upon your own experience, your observations of others, and your observations of Mr. Bacchus, do you have an opinion whether he was under the influence of alcohol the night that you arrested him?

A: Yes, I do.

Q: And what is that opinion?

A: He was very much under the influence of alcohol.

1.43 Describe the Story—Sample Dialogue

Q: What did you do on your Thanksgiving holiday three years ago?

A: My daughter, Molly, and I were going to be alone that day, and we were invited to go into the country for dinner at the home of some people with whom I work.

Q: What is their name?

A: Mr. and Mrs. Baskerville.

Q: How old was Molly at the time?

A: She was six.

Q: What time did you arrive?

A: We were invited for dinner at two p.m., and we arrived a few minutes after that as we got lost on the way.

Q: Had you ever been to the Baskervilles' home before that day?

A: No, I had not.

Q: What did you do when you got there?

A: Their farm is quite a long ways off the county road. We drove up the driveway and by the barn and parked in front of the house by the gate.

Q: Where is the barn located in relation to the house?

A: It is across the driveway.

Q: How far is the barn from the house?

A: About 100 feet.

Q: How far from the house did you park?

A: About 30 feet. There is a fence around the front yard, and we parked right by the fence.

Q: What did you do?

A: I got out of the car and waited for Molly to walk around the front of the car.

Q: What happened?

A: As Molly was walking in front of the car, something caught my attention out of the corner of my eye from the direction of the barn.

Q: What did you do?

A: I turned my head to see what it was.

Q: What did you see?

A: I saw an enormous shaggy brown dog running right towards Molly.

Q: Did it make any noise?

A: No, it was running real fast and was making no noise at all.

Q: How big was this animal?

A: It was huge. Its head was higher than my waist. It had a huge mouth, and I could see its teeth.

Q: What did you do?

A: I screamed and ran to Molly.

Q: What happened?

A: I grabbed her and started to pick her up and as I started to do that the beast leaped at us and bit Molly in the back of her neck.

Q: Go on.

A: We fell to the ground. I could not get my hand loose, and the dog was biting and snarling and tearing at us. There was blood all over, and we were both screaming and crying for help.

Q: What was the next thing that happened?

A: I heard a woman yelling.

Q: What did she say?

A: I heard something like, "Down Hound! Stop that! You naughty dog! You should be ashamed of yourself!"

Q: What did the dog do?

A: It let go and sat there snarling and growling at us.

Q: Did you see who the woman was?

A: Yes, Mrs. Baskerville.

Q: What did the dog look like?

A: It was a huge filthy hound. It had long, shaggy, matted brown hair covered with dirt. It smelled just awful. It had an enormous head with yellow eyes. It had huge teeth and was growling, drooling, and quivering as it sat there.

Q: What happened next?

A: Mrs. Baskerville took us inside the house and tried to stop the bleeding while her husband called an ambulance.

Q: Did she say anything to you?

A: She said that the darn dog was always jumping on people and that they should have locked the dog in the barn.

Q: Had she ever said anything to you about a dog before you came to the house that day.

A: Never! I never even knew that they had a hound.

1.44 Establish Conversations

The foundation needed to admit a relevant conversation is fairly easy when the conversation occurs face-to-face and the witness can identify the person making the statement. With telephone conversations, as the witness has to be able to identify the voice in order to show that the conversation relates to the case.

Sample Dialogues

Prior Familiarity with Voice:

Q: Did you conduct an investigation of the collapse of the ski lift gondola?

A: Yes, I did.

Q: What did you do?

A: I called up Stein Eriksson, the owner of the resort, on the telephone.

Q: Had you ever spoken to Stein Eriksson before?

A: Yes, many times.

Q: Did you recognize his voice when you called him?

A: Yes.

Q: How?

A: I recognized the sound of his voice and his accent.

Q: Did he identify himself to you in any other way?

A: Yes.

Q: How?

A: When he answered the phone he said, "Allo, dis is Stein Eriksson speking."

Q: Then what did he say?

A: He said, "I sure vish we had fixed da dern cable car."

Subsequent Identification of a Voice:

Q: What did you do on the fifth of January?

A: I called up a man to talk about the show.

Q: Did you talk to the man?

A: Yes.

Q: Did you know the man?

A: No.

Q: Did you recognize his voice?

A: No.

Q: Have you heard his voice since that conversation?

A: Yes.

Q: Where?

A: In the courtroom today when he testified for the plaintiff.

Q: How can you recognize his voice?

A: It is very distinctive—high pitched—and he has a silly laugh.

Q: What is the name of the man whose voice you heard today?

A: Peewee Herman.

Q: What did he tell you about the show when you phoned him?

A: He said that he wanted a prime time show.

Extrinsic Sources of Identification:

Q: Had you ever spoken to Groucho Marx before March 3 of last year?

A: No.

Q: Have you ever spoken to him since?
A: No.
Q: On March 3, what did you do?
A: First, I went to the city telephone book and looked up the phone number of Groucho Marx Productions.
Q: Then what?
A: I called the number and a woman answered "Groucho Marx Productions."
Q: What did you do?
A: I asked to speak to Groucho Marx.
Q: What happened?
A: First, there was silence, then the phone rang and a man answered and said, "Mr. Marx's office."
Q: What did you do then?
A: I asked to speak to Groucho Marx.
Q: And then?
A: A man answered and said, "Marx here, whadda ya want?"
Q: What did you say?
A: I identified myself and then asked him why he had shot the duck.
Q: What did he say?
A: He said, "You wodda too if you had the dumb thing flying down at you all the time."

J. HOW TO ASK QUESTIONS EFFECTIVELY

1.45 Ask Simple Questions

Simple, everyday conversational words are generally more effective as they are easy to understand. Complex, multi-syllable words or legalese sound snobbish, make it difficult to understand the testimony, and are boring. The ordinary language of the people in the community is most effective.

Sample Dialogues

Simple:

Q: Before the accident, where were you?

Complex:

Q: Prior to the accident, where were you situated?

Simple:

Q: Did you see something?

Complex:

Q: Did you have occasion to observe anything at all?

Simple:

Q: What happened on April 1?

Complex:

Q: Calling your attention to the date of April 1, what, if anything, occurred?

1.46 Ask Short Questions

Short questions make it easier for the lawyer to control testimony and to direct a witness to provide detail. Long, drawn out questions delay the testimony, waste time, and interrupt the flow of the testimony.

Sample Dialogue

Q: What were you doing?

A: I was the scorekeeper at the basketball game.

Q: Where were you?

A: I was sitting at mid-court at the scorer's table, about four feet back from the sideline.

Q: Who was playing?

A: Cannon Falls and Pine Island.

Q: What did you see shortly before the end of the first half?

A: I saw a man wearing a Pine Island jacket jump out of the bleachers and run right up and punch the coach of the Cannon Falls team right on the nose.

1.47 Ask Narrative and Specific Questions

The following examples demonstrate two comparative approaches to the development of a story: a story elicited with a narrative question and a story developed with specific questions.

(A) Sample Dialogue with Narrative Questions

Q: Tell us what you remember about that afternoon?

A: When the kids got home from school and had their snack, I sent them out to play. They had on light jackets and boots. The golf course across the street has a pond. The kids had skated there all winter. After they left, I thought they might head for it, so I went out looking for them. When I got to the pond, the ice had given way. I ran out to pull them from the water. I first got David on the shore and then I waded back into the water to find Mike. He was below the ice and I couldn't see him. I went under the ice as fast as I could and felt with my hands until I felt his arm. I grabbed him and pulled him out, and he was blue.

(B) Sample Dialogue with Specific Questions

Q: What is the first thing that happened when Amy and Mike came home from school on March 15?

A: They had a snack—crackers and milk.

Q: After the snack, what did they do?

A: They put on their play clothes and jackets to go outside.

Q: What kind of jackets?

A: Light, spring jackets.

Q: Why didn't they wear winter jackets?

A: Because it was a very mild day. The snow was melting.

Q: Where do the children like to play?

A: They like to play on the golf course in the winter because there are hills for sliding and a pond that they skate on.

Q: Where is the golf course?

A: Right across the road.

Q: On that day, did you tell them anything about the ice on the pond?

A: Yes.

Q: What?

A: I told them to stay off the ice because it was unsafe.

Q: After the children got dressed, what did they do?

A: They went outside.

Q: What did you do?

A: I thought they might head for the pond, so I went out looking for them.

Q: Did you see them?

A: No.

Q: What did you do?

A: I ran over to the pond and saw that the ice had broken through.

Q: What did you do?

A: I jumped into the water to find my kids.

1.48 Ask a Combination of Narrative and Specific Questions

An effective direct examination employs a mix of questions that call for short, narrative responses combined with short, controlled questions that elicit appropriate details. This mix of questions guides the witness in telling the story, permits the attorney to control the direction of the story, provides clarifying details, and holds the interest of the fact finder.

Sample Dialogue

Q: After the children got dressed, what did they do?

A: They went outside, and I saw them run towards the golf course.

Q: What did you do after you saw the children run towards the golf course?

A: I thought they might go to the pond, so I got dressed and ran after them. I was scared they would fall through the ice.

Q: Then what happened?

A: The ice had already given way, and both children were out of sight. I ran out to pull them from the water. I took my cardigan off and held one arm of the sweater and swung it out to David so that she could grab the other arm. I got her on the shore, and then I waded back into the water to Mike.

Q: Where was Mike?

A: He was below the ice, and I couldn't see him.

Q: What did you do?

A: I went under the ice as fast as I could and felt with my hands and after a little bit I felt his arm. I was so frightened.

Q: After you felt his arm, what did you do?

A: I grabbed him and pulled him out. I saw he was blue, and I cried for help.

1.49 Complete a Sequence

Sometime during an examination, the direct examiner realizes that something has been left out of an earlier part of the examination. In a rush to correct the problem and provide this information, the attorney may insert a question out of sequence.

Sample Dialogue

Q: What happened to you Ms. Belpre?

A: Well, the man attacked me. He was hitting and kicking me. I was yelling for help and trying to get away.

Q: By the way, I didn't ask you what time you got off work at the library that day. When did you get off work?

If the left out information is important, it should be introduced at the end of a segment, not in the middle.

1.50 Use Impact Words

A careful choice of impact words can have an effect on how testimony is perceived. Impact words are graphic words that vividly describe something in support of a perception the attorney is attempting to establish. The use of appropriate impact words helps the witness portray a persuasive and interesting story.

Neutral words:

Q: What was the **speed** of the two cars?

Impact words:

Q: How **slowly** were you driving?

Q: How **fast** was the other car going?

Neutral words:

Q: What was the **distance** between you and the other woman?

Impact words:

Q: How **close** were you to the other woman?

Q: How **far** away were you?

Neutral words:

Q: How **much** water was in the glass?

Impact words:

Q: How **full** was the glass?

Q: How **empty** was the glass?

1.51 Use Double Direct

Double direct is a technique in which part of a previous answer is used as a preface to the next question. This tactic repeats information so the fact finder hears the information twice, emphasizing important testimony. This technique should be reserved for important evidence.

Sample Dialogue

Q: When you finished studying, what did you do?

A: I went out to jog around the stadium.

Q: Which way did you go to get to the stadium?

A: I came off Arapahoe and headed toward the track.

Q: What time was that?

A: 6:00 p.m.

Q: What happened?

A: I jogged towards the track. When I got about 150 feet off Arapahoe, I passed a large hedge on my right. I heard branches scraping and twigs snapping.

Q: When you heard branches scraping and twigs snapping in the hedge, what did you do?

A: I ran faster.

Q: As you ran faster, what happened?

A: Someone ran out of the hedge onto the path and was running up behind me.

Q: How do you know?

A: I heard the running steps and then my arm was grabbed from behind and was twisted hard behind my back.

Q: What happened when your arm was twisted?

A: I lost my balance and fell into the hedge.

Q: When you fell into the hedge what happened?

A: The person put a knife to my throat.

1.52 Control the Answers and Correct Mistakes

The examiner must listen to every response carefully. Witnesses frequently misunderstand a question, make mistakes, or assume that the examiner wants an answer not called for by the question. It is often difficult to pay close attention to the answers for a variety of reasons. The direct examiner may be concerned about the next series of questions, the case, problems with opposing counsel, or other matters. Also, the advocate may be so familiar with the case and expect certain answers that when the witness says something different, the advocate may not hear it.

When a witness makes a mistake or does not answer the question precisely, the examiner must correct the witness. While it is usually not a good idea to interrupt a witness and break the flow of an examination, there will be occasions when the witness has made a factual mistake, or is rambling out of control, or has added information that is improper and the attorney must interrupt. Controlling the witness demonstrates that the examiner seeks only proper, responsive answers, bolstering the credibility of the witnesses and the examiner.

Sample Dialogue

Q: What did you see?

A: (*At a very rapid pace.*) There was this little old lady. She must have been seventy or eighty and she was walking towards me and she must have really been excited and I really thought that she was going to run into me and then she started talking to me and she said . . . .

Q: I am going to have to stop you right here for a moment. We are going to have to take it one step at a time. I'm going to ask you some simple questions and ask you to give a responsive answer. Okay?

A: Oh, yes.

Q: You can't tell us what the lady said to you because that's not allowed in this trial. Now when the lady spoke to you, were you looking at her face?

A: Yes.

A: Did you see if she was wearing glasses?

A: Yes, I did.

Q: Was she?

A: Yes, she was.

1.53 Explain Terms

The direct examiner should make sure the witness explains terms that have specialized or multiple meanings.

Sample Dialogue

Q: What did you do?

A: I examined the records using both the LIFO and FIFO accounting procedures.

Q: What does the term "LIFO" mean?

A: LIFO means last in, first out.

Q: And "FIFO"?

A: FIFO means first in, first out.

Q: Please explain those procedures in more detail, Mr. Descartes.

A: . . . .

1.54 Volunteer Weaknesses

Weaknesses in the witness' background or testimony may need to be briefly presented during the direct examination to minimize impact and to enhance the credibility of the witness and the attorney. Negative information about the witness or testimony that is not revealed on the direct examination and is first exposed on the cross-examination can be harmful. Weaknesses revealed on direct examination demonstrate that neither the examiner nor the witness has anything to hide, reducing the adverse affect of the weakness. In addition, the witness has the opportunity to explain the weakness in the witness' terms, not in the opposing counsel's words. Weaknesses should be addressed in a matter-of-fact way, and explained with as little embarrassment or concern as possible.

The decision to admit weaknesses can be difficult. If a weakness cannot be excluded by the rules of evidence, and the cross-examiner is expected to expose that weakness, the weakness may need to be brought out on the direct examination. At times it may be more effective to deal with a weakness on redirect examination in the hope that the cross-examiner will not bring up the matter or that the explanation will be so good that the cross-examination will appear foolish.

Sample Dialogue

Q: What color was the light?

A: Green.

Q: Did you talk with Lieutenant Columbo the day of the accident?

A: Yes.

Q: Did he write up a statement?

A: Yes, on a scrap of paper.

Q: Did that statement say the light was fuchsia?

A: Yes.

Q: Did you sign that statement?

A: Yes.

Q: Can you explain why you did that?

A: Yes, I can.

Q: Tell us please.

A: When Lt. Columbo was taking the statement, I was in the hospital and was in a lot of pain. I did not read the statement. I just signed it to get rid of him. He was always hanging around asking me questions. I did not realize that the statement said that the light was fuchsia.

1.55 Use Exhibits

Exhibits should be used in a way that enhances the testimony of a witness. The use of an exhibit in the structure of the examination should be carefully planned and an exhibit should reflect the purposes for which the witness is testifying. For example, a piece of real evidence such as a gun, contract, or broken machine part may be used most effectively when the witness first mentions or describes the evidence. Demonstrative evidence such as a diagram or photographs may be introduced at the stage of an examination when the witness explains those facts.

K. HOW TO CONDUCT A REDIRECT

The direct examiner has an opportunity to conduct a redirect examination after the completion of the cross-examination. Redirect examination provides the direct examiner with the opportunity to have the witness clarify or explain points raised on cross-examination and to cover new material raised by the cross-examination that was not dealt with on the direct examination. With proper preparation, the direct examiner can predict the areas of cross-examination and may cover those areas on direct examination and limit the effectiveness of a cross-examination. In addition, a redirect examination can be planned in advance so that the anticipated areas of weakness or vulnerability can be clarified or explained.

1.56 How Can You Ask?

The general rule is that redirect examination may only cover new material raised by the cross-examination. Redirect should not be used to go over the same information covered by the direct examination or raise new areas not covered by either the direct or cross-examinations.

Sample Dialogue

Cross-Examination of an Eyewitness:

Q: Have you ever seen someone you thought you recognized and waved at that person only to realize the person was a complete stranger?

A: Yes, that has happened to me.

Q: It was embarrassing to have that happen, wasn't it?

A: Well, yes it was.

Q: I have no further questions.

Redirect Examination of the Same Witness:

Q: Ms. Rashimka, when you thought you recognized a stranger, did that stranger stand two feet in front of you, face-to-face and demand all your money as the defendant did in this case?

A: Never. The only time I have been robbed is by that defendant.

1.57 What Should You Ask?

A well-prepared case and a good direct examination often make a redirect examination unnecessary. In making the decision whether to conduct a redirect examination, the following factors should be considered:

The witness may not have been prepared for certain redirect questions and should not be asked surprise questions.

The witness may not understand the point the attorney wants to make and misspeak.

Having the last word is not the most important thing. The same information need not be repeated over and over again just to get in the last word.

Continuing with redirect examination may add nothing to the information already provided.

Closing argument may be a much better time to explain the important parts of the case, rather than redirect examination.

Cases may be damaged by asking too many questions. A witness who repeats answers may look rehearsed, and mistakes can be made in regard to the same testimony.

Redirect examination gives the opponent the opportunity for a recross examination.

1.58 How Should You Ask?

The same rules of evidence apply to redirect and direct examination, with the same restrictions applying to the use of leading questions. There may be a greater latitude allowed in the use of leading questions during redirect in order to permit the examiner to focus on matters within the scope of the cross-examination and to speed the redirect to completion. Since the witness has testified on both direct and cross-examination, the redirect examiner may refer to previous answers and lead the witness to a specific topic through the use of this prior testimony. The opposing advocate may not object because the cross-examination consisted of leading questions, and may be so used to such questions that leading questions on the redirect may not sound improper.

1.59 How to Correct Mistakes and Refresh Recollection

Redirect examination may be used to refresh the witness' recollection if the witness has misstated or forgotten information during the cross-examination. See Fed.R.Evid. 612.

Sample Dialogue

Q: During the cross-examination you told us that the man held you by the throat with his left hand while he had a knife in his right. Are you sure that he had the knife in his right hand, Mr. Bowie?

A: Oh my, did I say right hand? I didn't mean to say that. He had the knife in his left hand and was choking me with his right.

Q: How do you know that?

A: Because I had grabbed his left hand so I wouldn't be knifed.

1.60 Should You Reserve the Introduction of Evidence?

Information should not be withheld during direct examination for later presentation during a redirect examination. A direct examiner who reserves important evidence runs the risk of not being able to present this important element of the case because the cross-examiner may not cross-examine at all or may not cover that particular area. There are some occasions where the delaying of the introduction of information is worth the risk of not being able to present the evidence at all. If the direct examination is structured in such a way so that the cross-examiner is very likely to cross-examine on the topic and damage will not be done to the case if the evidence is not dealt with, evidence may be reserved for redirect. If a topic was not covered either on the direct or the cross-examination, the direct examiner may be permitted to reopen the direct examination to permit the witness to be recalled to cover the new topic.

L. DIRECT EXAMINATION INFORMATION

This section presents several direct examination situations involving special considerations.

1.61 Former Testimony

In civil matters, testimony of a witness may be introduced through former testimony given at a deposition or another hearing. This testimony is either read or shown to the fact finder. Former testimony is admissible in lieu of live testimony if the previous testimony was given under oath, the witness is unavailable to testify at the trial, and the party against whom the testimony is offered had the opportunity to previously examine the witness, or another party with substantially the same interest or similar motive had that opportunity.

The most common use of former testimony in a civil matter involves the introduction of deposition testimony because the witness is unavailable. Depositions are commonly taken to preserve testimony when the offering advocate anticipates that witnesses will be unavailable. The deposition of such witnesses is taken and their testimony is recorded stenographically, or the deposition is videotaped. It is very common that the testimony of expert witnesses, who are unavailable because of their professional schedules, is presented by having their deposition testimony presented.

The procedure to introduce the former testimony is similar to the introduction of live testimony. The deposition transcript may be read with the direct examiner reading the questions and another person sitting in the witness stand supplying the answers. When this method is used the direct examiner should select a person to read the answers who looks credible and sounds persuasive to gain as much impact as possible from the reading of the deposition. It is easy to become bored when listening to the reading of a lengthy deposition transcript. The use of a videotape of the testimony presents the actual witness testifying and if correctly prepared, may be less boring.

Prior to the reading of the transcript or showing of the videotape, the opposing advocate may object to questions or answers contained in the former testimony. In court trials, arbitrations and administrative hearings the fact finder will need to review testimony, transcripts and video tapes in making a decision. In jury trials, the judge rules on each of the objections, and if sustained, the inadmissible question or answer is deleted. If a deposition transcript is read, the portions of the transcript ruled inadmissible are not read. If the videotape is used, the portions ruled to be inadmissible are not shown. There are a number of mechanical ways this can be done. An edited copy of the original tape can be made and shown. Or, the tape can be fast-forwarded to eliminate the inadmissible portions, or the monitor turned off, or the sound muted while the tape continues to play. Neither the written deposition transcript nor a videotape of the deposition go with a jury to the jury room during deliberations. This is to avoid the jurors giving such evidence more weight than other oral evidence heard by them from live witnesses during the trial.

Example (Deposition Transcript)

Examining Attorney: Your Honor, William Mayhew, an eyewitness, is unavailable to testify. Mr. Mayhew testified in a previous deposition. Both I and opposing counsel were present and examined him at that deposition. We now request permission of the court to read the deposition transcript of Mr. Mayhew to the jury.

Opposing Counsel: We have reviewed those parts of Mr. Mayhew's former testimony that the plaintiff plans to introduce, and we have no objection to the introduction of that evidence. After counsel for plaintiff completes the direct examination of Mr. Mayhew, we will introduce our cross-examination questions and answers.

Judge *(in a jury trial)*: Members of the Jury, at this time counsel for plaintiff will present to you the testimony of a witness who is unavailable to be here today to testify. You are to consider the testimony of this witness with the same degree of attention and consideration that you give the testimony of any other witness. Counsel, you may proceed.

Counsel: I will read the questions, your Honor, and a colleague from my firm, Elmer Gantry, will read the answers.

Court: Mr. Gantry, you may come forward and sit in the witness stand. Counsel, begin the questions and answers.

Example (Video Deposition)

Examining Attorney: Your Honor, Dr. Livingston, one of our expert witnesses, is unavailable to testify. We previously videotaped a deposition of his testimony, and counsel was present at that deposition. Your Honor has reviewed this videotape and has ruled on defendant's objections. Those questions and answers you ruled inadmissible have been edited from this videotape. We now request permission of the court to show to the jury the videotaped testimony of Dr. Livingston.

Judge: You may proceed.

In criminal cases, former testimony is usually inadmissible because the defendant has a constitutional right to be confronted by live witnesses and to cross-examine them. Former testimony in a criminal case may be admissible when there is a retrial of the same defendant, or if the defendant stipulates to its admissibility.

1.62 Past Recollection Recorded

When a witness has no present recollection and efforts to refresh recollection have failed or would fail, the introduction of past recollection recorded may be used to present evidence on direct examination. Federal Rule of Evidence 803(5) provides an exception to the requirement that a witness testify verbally.

The examiner will have prepared a witness for the use of past recollection recorded. It should not come as a surprise when a witness has no current recollection of an event. Statements introduced as past recollection recorded need to be marked and offered into evidence because they constitute the substantive evidence substituted for the verbal testimony of the witness. The foundation for the introduction of the recorded item includes:

The witness has no present, independent recollection.

The witness at one time personally knew information relevant to the case.

The information was written down or recorded by the witness at the witness' direction.

The writing or recording was created or adopted when the information was fresh in the witness' memory.

The writing or recording accurately contains the information.

The witness authenticates the exhibit.

Some witnesses (police, investigators, doctors, experts) may have to rely upon prior statements and reports to assist them during testimony. The opposing advocate may may want to object unless a proper foundation is laid.

Sample Dialogue

Q: What do you do for a living?

A: I'm a state highway trooper.

Q: How long have you been a state highway trooper?

A: Fifteen years.

Q: What are your primary duties?

A: To enforce highway traffic laws and to assist on highway accident scenes.

Q: Do you know how many tickets you generally give each year?

A: Approximately.

Q: How many?

A: Between twelve hundred and fifteen hundred a year.

Q: Do you remember the details of all the accident scenes you have investigated?

A: No.

Q: Do you remember the details of all the traffic tickets that you have written?

A: No.

Q: What is your procedure when you give a ticket?

A: After I give a ticket, I immediately write a report while sitting in my police car on the front and back of the ticket describing all the important details of the incident.

Q: Do you recall giving a ticket to the defendant in this case on June 1, last year?

A: Yes, I remember giving him a ticket.

Q: Do you remember the details of the incident?

A: Not completely.

Q: What do you remember?

A: I remember it was a drunk driving violation.

Q: Do you remember any other details?

A: No.

Q: How come?

A: Because I see so many drunk driving cases and speeding cases I cannot remember all the details.

To the Judge:

May I approach the witness?

Judge:

Yes you may.

Examining Attorney:

Q: Officer Estrada, I have just handed you what has been marked for identification as State's Exhibit No. 1. Do you recognize it?

A: Yes.

Q: What is it?

A: It is my copy of the ticket I was speaking about.

Q: Do you recognize it?

A: Yes I do.

Q: How?

A: I recognize my handwriting, my police number; I recognize the name of the defendant on it; and I recognize the date and time.

Q: Does reading this document, State's Exhibit No. 1 for identification, help refresh your recollection as to the details of the incident?

A: No it does not.

Q: Do you have any recollection of the details of that incident as you sit here today?

A: No I do not.

Q: At the time that you wrote down this report, did you remember the details of the incident?

A: Yes.

Q: When you wrote it down, did you write down the true and correct version of what you had observed?

A: Yes.

Q: Would you have signed it if it had not been a true and correct version of what you observed?

A: No, I would not have.

To the Judge:

At this time, I offer State's Exhibit No. 1 as past recollection recorded.

Judge:

Any objections, Counsel?

Opposing Counsel:

No objections.

Judge:

It is received.

Examining Attorney:

At this time, Officer, would you please read what you wrote down in the report.

A: Yes, I will: "I was proceeding on routine patrol in my police vehicle when I observed the subject vehicle, a new, bright red Ferrari, go past me on the right-hand shoulder at a very high rate of speed."

Q: Go on.

A: "At that time . . . ."

1.63 Witnesses With Communication Problems

A child or a witness with a communication problem requires special consideration as a witness. Often a child or mentally handicapped witness is the only person who can testify in such cases as child abuse, sexual assault, incest, neglect and dependency. Federal Rule of Evidence 611(c) permits leading questions to assist this witness in communicating. However, the more the attorney asks leading questions, the less competent the witness will appear to be and the less persuasive the testimony becomes.

A witness who has communication problems must be made to feel at ease in the courtroom. The preparation may require that the witness be brought into the room before the proceeding, rehearse testifying, and even be allowed to spend additional time to become comfortable with an unfamiliar and potentially scary place. A mix of leading and nonleading questions assists the witness in testifying, and helps lead up to critical testimony which should be given without the use of leading questions.

1.64 Character Evidence

Character evidence is evidence of a trait or characteristic of a person offered to prove that the person acted in conformity with such character. The evidence rules of almost all jurisdictions are consistent with the common law doctrine that character evidence is not admissible to prove that an individual acted in conformity with the individual's character on a specific occasion. Evidence of wrongs, bad acts, or crimes is generally inadmissible to prove that a party is a bad person or possesses a bad character. For example, evidence that a party has a trait for speeding while driving a car to prove that party was speeding is inadmissible. Conversely, evidence of good character, good deeds, or an exemplary life is inadmissible to prove that a party is a good person or possesses a good character. For example, proof that a defendant is a careful driver is inadmissible to prove that the defendant was not negligent. Character evidence may be relevant, but the unfair prejudice and confusion of the issues resulting from the character evidence outweighs the probative value of such evidence.

1.65 Character Evidence in Civil Matters

In a civil natter, character evidence is usually inadmissible to prove that the person acted in conformity on a particular occasion, but may be admissible in the following instances:

Evidence of the character of a person or a pertinent trait may be admissible to prove motive, opportunity, intent, preparation, plan, knowledge, identity, or absence of mistake or accident.

Evidence relating to the character for untruthfulness may be offered against the person testifying.

Evidence of the truthful character of a witness is admissible after the character of the witness for untruthfulness has been attacked.

If character is an issue or an element of liability or damages, evidence is admissible on that issue as in defamation cases (reputation of plaintiff).

1.66 Character Evidence in Criminal Cases

In criminal cases, character evidence is admissible in the following situations:

An accused may offer evidence of a pertinent personal trait. The defendant who claims self-defense in an assault case may offer evidence regarding the defendant's reputation for peacefulness.

The prosecution may offer character evidence to rebut the pertinent trait offered by the accused. In a self-defense case, the prosecutor can offer evidence of the defendant's reputation for violence.

The accused may offer evidence of a pertinent trait of the character of a victim and the prosecution may offer evidence in rebuttal.

The prosecution may offer evidence of a character trait of peacefulness of the victim in a homicide case to rebut evidence that the victim was the first aggressor.

Evidence relating to the character for untruthfulness may be offered against the person testifying.

Evidence of the truthful character of a witness is admissible after the character of the witness for untruthfulness has been attacked.

Character evidence may be admissible to prove motive, opportunity, intent, preparation, plan, knowledge, identity or absence of mistake or accident.

Character evidence which may be otherwise proper may be deemed inadmissible as unfairly prejudicial.

1.67 Introduction of Character Evidence

There are three ways in which character evidence may be introduced during direct examination of a witness:

(1) Opinion testimony: A witness may testify to a personal opinion about the character of a person if a foundation is first established concerning what the witness knows or has observed about the person over a period of time.

"I have personally known the defendant for 30 years, and I consider him to have an excellent reputation."

(2) Reputation testimony: A witness can testify to the reputation of a person in the community if a foundation is first established concerning what the witness has heard expressed about that person in a defined community. Reputation is the expressed community consensus about an individual.

"I have lived in the community for 30 years, and I have heard that the defendant's reputation is excellent."

(3) Specific instances of conduct: A witness may testify to first-hand knowledge about a person.

"The defendant has been a youth counselor and Red Cross volunteer for 10 years."

In all cases, character evidence is admissible by reputation testimony and opinion testimony. Federal Rule of Evidence 803(21) and similar state rules makes such testimony admissible hearsay. Testimony of specific instances of conduct is not admissible to prove character on direct examination. Specific instances of conduct may be more convincing, but such specific evidence also has the potential to arouse the greatest prejudice, to confuse the issues, and to consume unnecessary time. Reputation and opinion testimony are less convincing, less prejudicial, and take less time.

Where character evidence has been admitted on direct examination, specific instances of misconduct may be explored during cross-examination. A witness who testifies on direct examination that a party has good character may be cross-examined regarding knowledge about specific instances of bad character about that person. This line of inquiry may show that the witness may not have known about these specific instances, or ought not to be believed.

In cases in which a character trait of a person is an essential element of the case, proof of the trait may be made by specific instances of conduct. If a character trait is a direct issue in a case, then specific instances of good conduct may be introduced on direct examination to prove such issue. Specific instances of bad conduct may be raised on cross-examination to disprove such issue, and specific instances of bad conduct may be introduced on direct examination through a witness testifying on behalf of the adverse party to further disprove the character established. All questions regarding specific instances of good conduct or bad conduct must be asked in good faith and must be based on facts. Such situations may not be made up, may not be suggested by innuendo, or suggested by unsubstantiated questions.

Sample Dialogue (Direct Examination)

Q: How long have you lived in Washington?

A: 10 years.

Q: What do you do now?

A: I'm a consultant.

Q: Before you were a consultant, what did you do?
A: I was a senator.
Q: How long were you a senator?
A: Six years.
Q: Why did you quit being a senator?
A: I was defeated in an election.
Q: Do you know Congressman Doodle?
A: Yes.
Q: How long have you known him?
A: Ten years.
Q: Have you ever socialized with him?
A: Yes.
Q: How often?
A: At least once a month over the last ten years.
Q: Do you know other people in the Washington area who have socialized with Congressman Doodle?
A: Yes.
Q: How many?
A: Hundreds.
Q: Can you tell me some of the people that you know who have socialized with the Congressman?
A: Yes.
Q: Please tell us.
A: Other senators, representatives, employees of the House and Senate, and other consultants like myself.
Q: Have you ever talked to these people about Congressman Doodle's drinking habits?
A: Yes.
Q: How often?
A: Hundreds of times.
Q: Have you ever seen the Congressman drinking?
A: Yes.
Q: How many times?
A: On every occasion that I was with him.
Q: What is the most recent experience that you have had with the Congressman?

A: Last week.

Q: Based on your own observations and your discussions with others, do you know Congressman Doodle's reputation for sobriety in the community of Washington?

A: Yes, I do.

Q: What is that opinion?

A: Congressman Doodle's reputation is that he is a very sober person when he is not drinking.

1.68 Habit Evidence

Evidence of a particular habit of a person or the routine practice of an organization is admissible to prove that a person or organization acted in conformity with that habit on a particular occasion. Federal Rule of Evidence 406 does not define habit. Definitions may be found in treatises, statutes, or case law. Habit is generally defined as a regular response to a repeated specific situation. If the evidence of an otherwise relevant habit is unfairly prejudicial, an objection is proper and will be sustained.

M. COMPLEX CASES

1.69 Direct Examination in Complex Cases

Surveys of fact finders in cases involving many witnesses conclude that the fact finders like and prefer live witnesses to testimony produced by deposition transcript or videotape. The presence of real people adds human interest and drama to the case and makes it easier for the fact finders to remember and apply the evidence. Testimony produced by depositions often results in blah and uninteresting renditions of dull and unpersuasive evidence.

The order of the witnesses is also an important tactical decision. Witnesses with related or similar evidence should testify in a reasonable sequence. The order of testimony should match to the conclusions the attorney wants the fact finder to reach.

The use of exhibits is all the more critical in complex cases. The use of various types of exhibits can significantly enhance the testimony of a witness. The following chapter illustrates these uses.

N. WHAT YOU CANNOT ASK

This section describes improper uses of direct examination which are unethical and grounds for an objection, mistrial or new trial.

1.70 Facilitating the Presentation of Perjured Testimony

The knowing use of fraudulant, false or perjured testimony is prohibited. The direct examiner has a duty to prevent the misrepresentation of testimony. If a client in a criminal case insists on presenting false testimony, the attorney may be limited by constitutional considerations in determining how or if the problem may be revealed. A criminal defense lawyer may have to allow the defendant to testify but may not ask the witness any questions or use any false testimony as a part of the final argument. If an advocate knows that a witness, who is not a client, will offer perjured testimony, the advocate may not call that witness to testify.

An advocate may request to withdraw from the case, but the request may be denied. Denial of the request to withdraw usually occurs when the proceeding is well underway and the withdrawal will cause unfair delay which may cause prejudice to the opponent or the administration of justice.

1.71 Soliciting Inadmissible Responses

It is improper to solicit inadmissible responses. For example, it is highly improper for the direct examiner to ask, "Did you ever take photographs of that automobile before the repairs were made?" anticipating the witness will respond with, "No, but the insurance company did." A direct examiner must comply with the exclusionary rules of evidence and cannot attempt to prompt an inadmissible response from a witness, even with a question that is not objectionable.

1.72 Oops!

The inadvertant blurting out of inadmissible evidence by a witness can result in problems. The direct examiner should properly prepare the witness by explaining what information is inadmissible, and the impropriety of attempting to disclose inadmissible evidence.

1.73 Allowing the Client or Witness to Disrupt a Proceeding

Allowing a client to disrupt a proceeding may bring disciplinary action against the lawyer. Lawyers should not stand mute as their clients misbehave. Not only may the lawyer be sanctioned, but a client can be cited for contempt as well.

1.74 Using Tricks to Confuse Identification

The deliberate substitution of someone other than a party at the proceeding is improper. An advocate must disclose to the tribunal the names of the clients that the advocate represents. In a matter in which identification is an issue, it may be unethical to seat someone other than the client at counsel table for the purpose of eliciting an erroneous identification or to test an eyewitness' identification. However, full disclosure of the tactic beforehand may permit the use of this technique.

RESOURCES

Bibliography

Art of Advocacy: Direct Examination, Scott Baldwin (Matthew Bender 1981).

Calling Your Attention to the Direct Examination: How to Avoid The What Happened Next Question, Christine L. Hunt, 42 *Mercer L. R.* 619–626 (1991).

Delivering High-impact Direct Examination, E. John Wherry, Jr., 16 *Trial Diplomacy J.* 88–92 (1993).

Direct Examination, Michael H. Graham, 20 *Criminal L. Bulletin* 340–354 (1984).

Direct Examination (Examining Witnesses), J. Patrick Hazel, 14 *Litigation* 6 (1987).

Direct Examination—The Forgotten Advocacy Tool, Herbert J. Stern, 6 *Amer. J. of Family L.* 268 (1992).

Direct Examination: Lawyers Need to Prepare Both Witnesses and Themselves, John P. Bracken, 23 *Trial* 63 (1987).

Direct Examination—Refreshing Recollection, Exclusion and Separation of Witnesses, Michael H. Graham, 20 *Criminal L. Bulletin* 430–441 (1984).

Direct Examination: Some Evidentiary and Practical Considerations, W. Dent Gitchell, 9 *Univ. of Arkansas at Little Rock L. J.* 255–301 (1986).

Direct Examination of Fact Witnesses: Where Counsel Can Best Make the Case, Harvey Weitz, 25 *Trial* 107 (1989).

Direct Examination of Lay Witnesses, Russ M. Herman, 24 *Trial* 77 (1988).

Direct Examination Questions (child custody), Gary N. Skoloff, 4 *Family Advocate* 42–44 (1982).

Examination of Witnesses, Richard A. Gonzales (Callaghan 1989–).

The Gentle Art of Conversational English in Direct Examination, Carol B. Anderson, 14 *Amer. J. of Trial Ad.* 111–132 (1990).

The Heart of a Trial: Direct Examination (Trial Techniques: Tools of the Trade), Deanne C. Siemer, 28 *Trial* 48–53 (1992).

How to Prepare and Conduct a Direct Examination of a Witness, Leonard Packel, 28 *The Practical Lawyer* 74 (1982).

Leading Questions Permitted During Direct Examination of Child Witness, Alec Bramlett, 38 *South Carolina L. R.* 127–129 (1986).

More on Direct Examination, James W. McElhaney, 8 *Litigation* 43 (1981).

Organizing Direct Examination, James W. McElhaney, 76 *ABA J.* 92 (1990).

Questioning Techniques and Tactics, Jeffrey L. Kestler (Shepard's/McGraw-Hill 1982–).

Redirect Examination; How to Make the Most of It, Louis W. Breck and Mark F. Howell, 23 *Trial* 69 (1987).

Refreshing Recollection (refreshing a witness's recollection), James W. McElhaney, 77 *ABA J.* 86 (1991).

A Strategy for Effective Use of the Courtroom During Direct Examination, Jeff Wolfe, 10 *Amer. J. of Trial Ad.* 95–108 (1987).

Specific Cases/Witnesses

The Child Witness: Techniques for Direct Examination, Cross-examination, and Impeachment, John E. Myers, 18 *Pacific L. J.* 801–942 (1987).

Direct Examination of the Child Witness, Dixie A. Morrow, 27 *Air Force L. R.* 97–104 (1987).

Direct Examination Techniques for the Criminal Defense Attorney, Mark J. Kadish and Rhonda A. Brofman, 3 *Trial Diplomacy J.* 6 (1980).

Video

Art of Advocacy Skills in Action Series: Direct Examination, Matthew Bender & Co., Inc. (1981).

The Basics of Direct Examination, Trial Practice, Anderson Publishing (1990).

Direct and Comparative Cross Examination, National Institute For Trial Advocacy (1976).

Direct and Cross Examination of a Party in a Civil Case, National Institute For Trial Advocacy (1978).

Direct and Cross Examination in a Civil Case, National Institute For Trial Advocacy (1979).

Direct and Cross Examination of the Defendant in a Criminal Case, National Institute For Trial Advocacy (1977).

Direct and Cross Examination of a Witness in a Criminal Case, National Institute For Trial Advocacy (1976–1977).

Direct and Cross Examination of a Rape Victim in a Criminal Case, National Institute For Trial Advocacy (1976–1977).

Direct and Three Comparative Cross Examinations of a Major Prosecution Witness in a Federal Narcotics Case, National Institute For Trial Advocacy (1976–1977).

Direct Examination, National Institute For Trial Advocacy (1983).

Film

Presumed Innocent (1990).

Suspect (1987).

Jagged Edge (1985).

Kramer vs. Kramer (1979).

Oh, God (1977).

Anatomy of a Murder (1959).

Witness for the Prosecution (1957).

Miracle on 34th Street (1947).

*

CHAPTER 2
CROSS–EXAMINATION

All true glory, while it remains true, holds it. It is the maintaining of truth that is so hard.

— Elizabeth Goudge

A. SCOPE

2.01 Types of Cross-Examination

Cross-examination is the process of examining an opposing party or adverse witness. The purpose of cross-examination is to obtain information necessary to support statements made in summation. The goal of cross-examination is to reveal information that supports the cross-examiner's case and that damages the opposing party's case. There are two types of cross-examination:

Supportive cross.

Cross-examination can develop evidence that supports the cross-examiner's case. Questions may be asked on cross-examination to elicit favorable information not developed on direct examination and to repeat or bolster favorable evidence.

Discrediting cross.

Cross-examination can discredit the testifying witness or another witness. This may be accomplished in several ways, including attacking the credibility of the witness or testimony. Most of the questions asked on cross-examination are designed to reduce the persuasive value of the opposition's evidence.

2.01.1 Supportive Cross-Examination

Supportive cross-examination seeks to develop information helpful to the cross-examiner's case. The nature of the favorable information depends, naturally, upon the particular facts of a case. Several considerations help in determining whether the witness has favorable information that ought to be elicited on cross-examination.

WHAT STATEMENTS to be made in summation rely upon the testimony of this witness? If a witness is the only source of helpful information, that evidence must be elicited during cross-examination. For example, if a witness is the only person who can identify a signature on a document, then that witness must be asked questions authenticating that document.

WHAT ADMISSIBLE evidence does the witness know? A review of the knowledge a witness has may reveal information that supports the cross-examiner's case which ought to be elicited through cross-examination. For example, if a witness has personal knowledge of the identity of individuals present during a conversation, the witness can be required to identify those individuals.

WHAT ADMISSIONS has the witness made? If a witness has made written or oral statements, these admissions ought to be reviewed to determine which of them might be helpful to the cross-examiner's case. For example, in a breach of contract case, discovery may produce an admission that the opposing party failed to make an installment payment on time. One way to introduce this admission is to ask the opposing party about it on cross-examination.

WHAT INFORMATION does the witness have to corroborate favorable evidence? An opposing witness may have information to support a favorable fact established by another witness. Cross-examination can produce corroborating testimony which may be more persuasive because it is obtained from an adverse witness.

CAN THE WITNESS bolster or rehabilitate the credibility of favorable witnesses? In addition to introducing proof of a fact through an adverse witness, testimony of that witness corroborating the testimony of a favorable witness may increase the credibility of the favorable witness. For example, if the testimony of a husband testifying in support of his wife can be corroborated by the opposing party, the credibility of the husband is enhanced.

WHAT PORTIONS of the direct examination were helpful? Direct examination often contains some information that bolsters the cross-examiner's case. Helpful testimony from direct examination may be repeated and expanded on cross-examination. For example, an eyewitness called by a plaintiff who observed a traffic accident which occurred during a rainstorm can be asked questions on cross-examination to establish poor visibility and slick roads.

2.01.2 Discrediting Cross-Examination

The purpose of discrediting cross-examination is to show that the testimony developed on direct examination and evidence introduced by the opposing party is inaccurate, incomplete, inconsistent, implausible, improbable, impossible, or unbelievable. Discrediting cross-examination undermines the other side's case and reduces the credibility of the other side's witnesses. It is highly unlikely that the other side's case or the credibility of a witness will be totally discredited on cross-examination. More likely, bits and pieces of damaging information will be revealed that gradually erode the opponent's case. The basic goal of discrediting cross-examination is to discredit evidence or impeach a witness.

2.02 Your Risks With Cross-Examination

Cross-examination should be conducted with realistic expectations and with an assessment of the inherent risks. Cross-examination will not necessarily "win" a case or work miracles. Risky questions that have little hope of obtaining helpful information are often asked out of desperation because the cross-examination is not well conceived. Most of the risks involved in cross-examination arise because the witness is adverse, hostile or uncooperative. These risks can be reduced or eliminated by asking proper questions. Non-leading questions that do not control the witness are risky and should not be asked. Examples include open ended questions that permit a witness to explain, questions that ask how or why, questions that are asked out of curiosity with no expectation of what the answer will be, and long, confusing questions.

2.03 The Need for a Good Faith Basis

An advocate must have a good faith basis for cross-examination questions and cannot ask a question on cross-examination unless the advocate has proof of the underlying facts. These must be a source of reliable information—a possible witness or document that supports the statement made on cross. For example, a cross-examiner cannot ask a witness, "You drank ten beers that evening, right?" unless there is available direct or circumstantial evidence to prove that statement. That rationale for this requirement is to prevent the cross-examiner from suggesting false facts through leading questions. While a cross-examiner cannot fabricate innuendos or inferences on cross-examination, and must have proof of the facts underlying the questions, the proof may not be or need not necessarily be actually admitted as evidence.

2.04 Common Myths About Cross-Examination

There are a number of myths about cross-examination that arise from a misunderstanding of cross-examination strategies and tactics. An explanation of some of these myths may clear up some of the misconceptions.

MYTH: Only an experienced advocate can be an effective cross-examiner.

An advocate who thoroughly prepares and properly asks cross-examination questions can be effective. All advocates, regardless of experience, have the capability to conduct an effective cross-examination.

MYTH: The cross-examiner need not be caring or sensitive.

The fact finder may identify with the witness. The witness may be perceived as a nice, decent person or may have a background similar to the background of the fact finder. Witnesses should ordinarily be treated courteously and respectfully, and not treated in an uncaring or insensitive manner.

MYTH: Cross-examination should be conducted very aggressively.

An advocate who conducts an aggressive cross-examination may be perceived as manipulating the witness and the evidence. An advocate must be perceived as fair and should be politely insistent and assertive rather than overly aggressive. Some witnesses and some situations may permit an aggressive approach, but this technique is inappropriate for most witnesses.

MYTH: The witness must be destroyed on cross-examination.

The purpose of cross-examination is not necessarily to make the witness look or feel bad, but to obtain information to win a case. After a good cross-examination, a witness may leave the stand without feeling "destroyed."

MYTH: The witness should always be shown to be a liar.

Attacking the credibility of witnesses by suggesting or inferring that they are lying is ill-advised unless there is direct evidence of their lie. Most witnesses make honest and good faith efforts to describe an event. They will neither look like nor sound like they are making things up. However, it is not uncommon for witnesses who see or hear only a portion of an incident to add details they assume occurred. These witnesses may then blend their recollection of what actually occurred with the assumed details. This mistaken recollection and belief forms the basis for their testimony.

MYTH: Cross-examinations must produce dramatic results.

Cross-examination is only one part of the process. A cross-examination that does not leave the fact finder gasping or the witness crying does not indicate that the cross-examination has been ineffective. Some cases may involve such dramatic moments, but most do not.

MYTH: Cross-examination is an opportunity to debate with the witness.

Argumentative questions are improper and likely to draw an objection. The cross-examiner wants to obtain "yes" or "no" responses from a witness and wants to avoid debating with the witness.

MYTH: Cross-examination often escalates into a shouting match between the witness and the cross-examiner.

There is no need for an advocate to ask questions in a loud or harsh manner, except in unusual circumstances. Few witnesses deserve or require this treatment.

MYTH: Cross-examination should result in the witness "confessing."

Seldom will witnesses "confess" their guilt or liability on the stand, certainly not with the frequency that Perry Mason achieved such results. If they do, call us (collect) and we'll include it in our next edition.

MYTH: Cross-examinations that appear on television or in the movies are realistic and appropriate.

More often than not, cross-examination questions asked in a television program or motion picture are unrealistic and inappropriate. A witness seldom knows extraordinarily damaging information and rarely deserves to be treated in the way depicted in television and the movies.

MYTH: Cross-examinations should always be short.

A cross-examination should be as long as necessary to obtain the required information from the witness. With some witnesses, cross-examination will be short. With other witnesses, cross-examination may be relatively long. There is no set time limit for effective cross-examinations. The facts, witnesses, and circumstances determine the content and length. While a lengthy, rambling cross-examination may be very ineffective, one that is too short may fail to establish necessary or useful evidence.

MYTH: Cross-examination should cover one point, and no more than a few points.

Some advocates suggest that cross-examination should only cover one or a few points. This is appropriate advice if that's all the information a cross-examiner needs to develop. Many cross-examinations require the development of more points. What one cross-examiner considers to be one point with six subpoints, another may consider to be six points. Regardless of the semantics or the counting system used, a cross-examination should cover those points needed to be used in summation.

MYTH: Cross-examination is the most difficult skill.

Different advocates have different views about which part of the case is most difficult. A well-prepared cross-examination, seeking answers already known by the cross-examiner, need not be any more difficult than other parts of the case. Cross-examination can become very difficult and very damaging if questions are phrased improperly, inappropriate areas are explored, or the attorney loses control over the witness. These problems can be reduced or eliminated with proper planning and presentation.

B. HOW TO PREPARE

2.05 Planning

The preparation of a cross-examination begins early in a case and continues until the moment cross-examination begins. The cross-examiner listens carefully to the answers the witness gives on direct examination and adds, deletes or modifies questions to be asked during cross.

After the witness has testified on direct, the cross-examiner is usually able to ask a high percentage of the prepared questions. This occurs because the well-prepared cross-examiner already knows or anticipates what the witness knows and does not know. Modifications may be necessary, but the number of revisions can be reduced by thorough planning.

Adjustments may also be necessary during the cross-examination itself. The witness may not respond as anticipated, or may give unresponsive or rambling answers. The advocate must listen carefully during the cross and flexibly adapt to the responses by asking follow-up questions that produce the desired responses.

2.06 Should There be a Cross-Examination?

The decision to cross-examine must be made both before and again during the case, immediately after the witness has testified. The vast majority of witnesses merit some cross-examination questioning. Whether cross-examination should be conducted as planned, or whether any cross-examination should be conducted at all, are questions that must be finally resolved after the witness has completed direct examination. The following factors should be considered in determining whether a witness should be cross-examined:

Has the witness damaged the case? If the witness has not provided any evidence which damages the case, the cross-examination may not be necessary. A witness who did not appear credible, or whose story is not credible, or who has been contradicted by other evidence may not need to be cross-examined.

Is the witness important to the other side? The more significant a witness is to the opposing side, the more likely it is that cross-examination will be necessary.

Will the fact finder expect cross-examination? Witnesses who have provided damaging information or who are important to the other side will probably need to be cross-examined to avoid the fact finder misperceiving the decision not to cross-examine and to prevent the opposition commenting on such failure during summation.

Did the witness omit important adverse information on direct examination? If the witness left something significant out on direct examination, cross-examination regarding that information may be unwise as that information may then be disclosed for the first time on cross or redirect examination. Occasionally, an opponent may intentionally withhold evidence during the direct examination of a witness anticipating the evidence will be disclosed on cross-examination or redirect. If there is no cross-examination regarding this evidence, this information may never be disclosed. Some experienced direct examiners set this trap for the inexperienced cross-examiner.

Will cross-examination unavoidably bring out information that is harmful to the case? If cross-examination will yield more harmful information than helpful information, it will be best not to cross-examine.

Are questions being asked only for the sake of asking questions? If the cross-examination will serve no better purpose, than it ought not to be conducted.

Does this witness present any difficulties that may cause substantial problems? If a witness is very difficult to control or some other problem exists, the decision to cross-examine should be reconsidered.

2.07 Full and Fair Opportunity to Cross-Examine

A party has a right fully and fairly to cross-examine a witness. Unusual situations may arise when a witness who has testified on direct examination cannot be completely cross-examined. These situations include: (1) the assertion of a privilege by the witness which properly permits the witness to refuse to answer questions, (2) a witness becoming ill or otherwise incapacitated before or during cross-examination, and (3) the refusal of a witness to answer a question. In these situations, the cross-examiner may request that the direct examination testimony of the witness relating to the cross-examination topics be stricken because no opportunity exists to cross-examine the witness regarding those matters.

2.08 What is the Scope of Cross-Examination?

The scope of cross-examination is usually limited to the following two areas: the subject matter of direct examination and matters affecting credibility issues. See Fed.R.Evid. 611. Judges and arbitrators have discretion to permit inquiries into additional matters. Most judges provide cross-examiners with reasonable latitude to explore relevant areas which affect the case or the credibility of a witness. While the rules of a given jurisdiction may appear to restrict the scope of cross-examination, actual practice often permits broad inquiries.

If an area of inquiry on cross-examination exceeds the scope of the direct examination and does not involve credibility issues, the cross-examiner has several options. First, the questions may be asked and the opponent may not object. Second, the question may be asked, the opponent may object, and the objection may be overruled, permitting the answer. Third, the cross-examiner can seek permission to allow a broader cross-examination. In this case, the advocate may explain that the witness could be called back later to testify, and it would be more efficient if the examination was completed at one time. Fourth, the advocate can subsequently call the witness during the cross-examiner's next opportunity to introduce affirmative evidence.

2.09 Preparing Topics and Written Questions in Advance

Cross-examination is most effective when topics and questions are prepared in advance. Experienced advocates may be able to effectively cross-examine by relying solely on a list of topics. Many advocates, however, especially those who are inexperienced, need to write out questions to be most effective. Effective cross-examination often demands precise questions that contain particular words. The extent to which written questions should be prepared depends upon the nature of the question, the significance of the topic, the type of witness, and the experience and ability of the advocate. Most prepared questions will not need to be altered significantly during the case, but a cross-examiner must adapt the questions to changing circumstances. The advocate should avoid simply reading prepared questions and must pay attention to the witness' verbal and nonverbal responses in order to ask follow-up, clarifying or additional questions.

2.10 How Should Cross be Structured?

Cross-examination questions ought to be asked in an order that makes the cross-examination most interesting, persuasive, and memorable. An effective way to determine and select the sequence of cross-examination points is to:

List all the points expected to be made.

Divide the points into the two broad categories of cross-examination: supportive cross and discrediting cross.

Within these categories, **rank** each point from most to least important.

Of the more important points, **decide** which should begin and which should end the cross-examination segment.

Organize the other points in a sequence that best serves the needs of the particular cross-examination.

Select and **structure** any subtopics under the main points.

Review all the listed points and determine whether the initial assessment of their rank, order, and sequence appears to be the most effective.

2.11 Order of Cross

If both categories of cross-examination questions—supportive and discrediting—are to be asked, the supportive cross-examination questions ought to be asked first for a number of reasons. These questions elicit helpful information and will be emphasized by being asked at the beginning of the cross-examination. And these questions follow the pattern of questions asked on direct examination, which was just completed. The witness will be more likely to be more cooperative at the beginning of such a cross-examination, and the credibility of the witness has not yet been attacked, and the witness may be perceived to be more believable.

The order of the supportive cross-examination questions should follow a prepared structure, with important questions beginning and ending the line of questioning, and with the other points asked in the middle. The final point of supportive cross-examination should also serve as a transition into the discrediting category of cross-examination.

The shift from supportive to discrediting cross-examination may cause a problem. The cross-examiner wants the fact finder to believe the admissions elicited during the supportive cross-examination and to disbelieve the witness during discrediting cross-examination. With some witnesses, it might be advisable to omit or restrict the scope of the discrediting cross-examination to avoid the witness from being entirely discredited. The transition questions that begin the discrediting cross-examination should be selected to reduce this problem. With other witnesses, the discrediting cross-examination may render testimony so unbelievable that the fact finder will not believe the supportive cross-examination answers. In these situations, it may be better to avoid asking supportive cross-examination questions altogether, unless there is no other source for this information.

The order of the discrediting cross-examination questions should also follow a prepared structure. Important points should be made at the beginning and the end of this category of questions, with other points interspersed in the middle.

An alternative to a logical sequence of planned questions is to probe areas in a random fashion. This "jumping around" approach has the advantage of causing problems for witnesses who may be fabricating their responses. Such a witness, if asked questions in a logical or chronological order, may be able to maintain the fabrication, but if asked questions in a random order may be more likely to testify inconsistently. This approach has some disadvantages. The cross-examiner may have difficulty in remembering what has been asked, and the fact finder may find it difficult to follow an unstructured cross-examination. To be effective, this approach requires a lot of practice or experience.

2.12 How Should Cross be Concluded?

The concluding questions of a cross-examination should have the following characteristics: the questions should conclude the examination on a high note by making an effective point, should not be objectionable because sustained objections disrupt the conclusion, and should be of the type the witness will respond to favorably. If the cross-examiner has a doubt regarding whether a series of questions are effective, they should not be used for the conclusion. "Safe" questions ought to be used for the conclusion, and risky questions asked earlier.

2.13 Recross Examination

The scope of recross examination is limited to the subject matter of the redirect examination. The purpose of conducting a recross is the same as conducting a cross-examination: Is there any information this witness has that is needed for summation? Recross examination questions usually refer to the previous redirect answers of the witness and compare these responses to contradictory evidence. There often is no need to conduct a recross, and a recross should not be conducted merely because redirect questions were asked. Recross questions should not be asked if the redirect was ineffective or if the examination of the witness has been overly lengthy, and the fact finder cannot absorb more information from this witness.

2.14 Where to Cross

The cross-examiner should be visible during the examination. Unlike direct examination, when the direct examiner may be inconspicuous, the cross-examiner should be conspicuous.

The cross-examiner may have an option whether to sit or stand. Many jurisdictions require the cross-examiner to stand behind a lectern and not move about the courtroom. Other jurisdictions require that the advocate remain seated behind counsel table. Typically, cross-examiners may approach the witness when showing the witness an exhibit or using a visual aid, and are typically allowed to be close to a witness who has a hearing impairment or other disability that makes communication difficult.

In jurisdictions where the advocate has an option to stand and move around the courtroom, the cross-examiner should determine what location is best. This will depend upon the nature of the questions asked and the demeanor and responses of the witnesses. If the cross-examiner wants the fact finder to be able to observe the witness displaying guilt or uncertainty, the cross-examiner should stand in a location which requires the witness to look in the direction of the fact finder. If the cross-examiner can move during cross-examination, movement should be made with a purpose and should not be random. It may be effective to move closer to the witness during impeachment or when significant questions are asked to control the response of the witness.

2.15 "Uncross" Demeanor

An advocate who appears confident and composed will make the cross-examination more effective and persuasive. If the witness perceives that the cross-examiner is confident, the witness is more likely to answer questions directly and be less evasive. The most effective demeanor for a cross-examiner is to be firm, yet sensitive. This is especially true during the beginning of a cross-examination attempting to elicit supportive evidence. A "friendly" cross-examiner is more likely to elicit favorable information. Some witnesses deserve special treatment, including sympathetic witnesses such as young children, a victim of a crime, or a bereaved spouse.

Other situations may require more assertiveness on the part of the cross-examiner, particularly during impeachment efforts or when controlling an evasive or rambling witness. The cross-examiner should avoid becoming combative with the witness and avoid displays of anger. Such conduct often makes thinking difficult and will likely draw objections.

2.16 Tactical Considerations

Effective cross-examination requires the use of proper tactics and techniques. Many of these approaches are principles which should not be violated. All of these approaches are matters which need to be considered before and during the presentation of a cross.

Form of the question

Content of the question

Seeking agreement with the witness

Controlling the witness' responses

Emphasizing points

Utilizing safe questions

Questions for specific witnesses

The categories are not listed in any order of importance or priority because the facts, issues, and witness to be cross-examined determine which approaches are most useful. Not all of the techniques ought to be used in every cross, but many of them will be applicable. If a problem does occur during cross, it will usually be because one of the tactics was not properly employed.

Cross-examination questions must be carefully crafted. The difference between an effective cross-examination question and an ineffective one is often very subtle. A witness may properly refuse to answer a question, may rightfully claim a question is unclear, and may try to explain an answer, all because the cross-examiner failed to ask a precise and proper question.

C. FORMING QUESTIONS

2.17 Lead the Witness

Only questions that suggest or contain the answer should be asked on cross. Questions that require a "yes," "no," or short, anticipated answers should be asked so the testimony develops as anticipated. The question "why" and questions which require explanations should be avoided, because they call for open-ended answers that will reveal unnecessary information and cannot be controlled.

Sample Dialogue

Q: You are Chicago, correct?
A: Yes.
Q: You are hog butcher for the world?
A: Yes.
Q: Toolmaker, correct?
A: Yes.
Q: You are also a player with railroads and the nation's freight handler?
A: Yes.
Q: It is fair to say you are stormy?
A: Yes.
Q: Brawling?
A: Yes.
Q: You are the city of the big shoulders?
A: Of course.

A proper question requires the witness to respond "yes" or "no." An improper question permits the witness to describe, expand or explain the answer.

2.17.1 Form of Leading Question

Leading questions should be formulated in a way that prompt responsive answers. An effectively phrased leading question requires the witness to agree with the question. The more the question suggests the answer, the more effective it will be.

Ask: You saw Charlie Allnut on the African Queen?

Not: Did you see the defendant on the African Queen?

Modifying phrases or words may be added to leading questions to prompt an answer. The repetitive use of a single phrase ought to be avoided, however, because it may detract from the substance of the question.

Examples

You saw the defendant on the boat, isn't that true?

or

It is true that you saw the defendant on the boat?

or

The defendant was on the boat, correct?

or

It is true that you saw the defendant on the boat?

Leading "questions" may also be asked in the form of statements which sound like questions because of the cross-examiner's voice inflection.

Sample Dialogue

Q: You met Buddy Holly at the airport?

A: Yes.

Q: At about 11:00 p.m.?

A: Yes.

Q: That was the first time you met Mr. Holly?

A: Yes.

Q: And the last?

A: Yes.

The various forms of leading questions ought to be used during a cross-examination for variety and to prevent a cross from sounding monotonous.

2.18 Use Simple, Short Questions

Short, straightforward questions in simple, understandable language are most effective. Lengthy or rambling questions will be confusing.

Ask:

Q: The fight began?

A: Yes.

Q: The referee stood in the middle of the ring?

A: Yes.

Q: Ali stood in one corner?

A: Yes.

Q: Frazier stood in the opposite corner?

A: Yes.

Q: Ali began to move toward the center of the ring?

A: Yes.

Q: Frazier also began to move towards the middle of the ring, right?

A: Yes.

Not:

Q: As the fight began both Ali and Frazier stood in their respective corners and then each of them began to move towards the center of the ring, isn't that what happened?

2.19 Avoid Multiple Negative Questions

Questions that contain double or multiple negatives are misleading and should not be asked.

Examples

Q: It is correct is it not, that you don't know who was on the Galactica?

Q: It is not true, is it, that you are not an alien?

D. COMPOSING QUESTIONS

2.20 Ask Factual Questions

Questions which include facts prompt responsive answers. The factual words included in the cross-examination question must be based on accurate information to force a witness to admit the accuracy of the question. Questions which seek a conclusion may permit the witness to be non-responsive or explain an answer.

Avoid asking:

Q: When you visited Michael Cory, you wanted to sell him as much insurance as you could?

A: He came to my office. I told him I could provide him with an insurance policy that met his needs.

Instead ask:

Q: You asked Mr. Cory to come to your office?

A: Yes.

Q: While he was in your office, he told you he needed insurance coverage?

A: Yes.

Q: You told him you could provide him with insurance?

A: Yes.

Q: You wanted to sell him insurance?

A: Yes.

Some words may appear to be "facts" but are conclusory words. Each cross-examination question should be reviewed to determine whether the precise words used are facts or whether they include elements seeking a conclusion.

Avoid asking:

Q: Mr. Churchill read the lease agreement, correct?
A: He may have skimmed the lease.
Q: He understood the terms of the lease, didn't he?
A: I don't know.

Instead ask:

Q: You handed Mr. Churchill the lease agreement?
A: Yes.
Q: You saw him look at the lease agreement?
A: Yes.
Q: He sat there for some time looking at the lease?
A: Yes.
Q: The two of you discussed the lease for over an hour?
A: Yes.
Q: He asked you some questions about the lease?
A: Yes.
Q: You answered his questions?
A: Yes.
Q: You asked him if he had any other questions about the ease?
A: Yes.
Q: You asked him whether that lease met his country's needs?
A: Yes.
Q: And he said, "Yes it did?"
A: Correct.
Q: He signed that lease?
A: Yes.

2.21 Properly Ask for Opinions

An effective way to force a witness to provide an opinion is to first establish the factual basis for the opinion. For example, if you want eyewitnesses to admit they were tired at the time they made an identification, you first need to establish the factual basis for their being tired before asking them the question about their being tired.

Sample Dialogue

Q: Mr. Chaplin, your wallet was stolen at approximately 8 p.m., correct?
A: Yes.
Q: You got up that morning about 6 a.m.?
A: Approximately 6 o'clock.
Q: You worked from 8 a.m. until 7 p.m.?
A: Yes.
Q: You worked hard during parts of the day.
A: Sure.
Q: Your normal work day is from 8 a.m. until 5 p.m., correct?
A: Yes.
Q: You worked later than usual that day, right?
A: Yes.
Q: Working 11 hours that day was a tiring experience?
A: Yes.
Q: You were naturally tired at the end of your work day?
A: Yes.
Q: You were going home and looking forward to resting?
A: Sure.
Q: Because you had a very tiring day at the office, right?
A: I was tired.

If the witness were asked the opinion question before being asked the previous factual questions, the witness may have tried to bring up reasons for not being tired. Even if the witness refused to admit to being tired at the end of the day, the fact finder would believe the witness ought to have been tired and would not believe the witness' claim he was not tired.

2.22 Use Modifiers

The use of adjectives and adverbs as modifiers may help in obtaining favorable responses from a witness. Different impressions may be created on cross-examination if appropriate modifying words or phrases are used. For example, a witness may be willing to admit to different degrees of being tired depending on the sequence of questions asked and the modifying words used.

Sample Dialogue

Q: You were somewhat tired after working a full day, correct?

A: Yes.

Q: Working all those hours made you feel tired?

A: Yes.

Q: Working those additional overtime hours made you more tired than usual?

A: Perhaps.

Q: The hard and stressful day you had made you feel quite tired at the end of the day?

A: Yes.

Further questioning with some witnesses may have them agreeing to being "very tired" at the end of the day. Using various modifiers—a little, somewhat, quite, very—is an effective way to have the witness gradually agree to a position.

2.23 Use Synonyms

If a specific word is being sought on cross-examination, a synonym may be useful instead of trying to force the witness to admit to one specific word. A thesaurus provides alternative words that more effectively describe a situation. In the eyewitness example, having the witness agree to being "exhausted" at the end of the day rather than just being "tired" is more effective. Consider using synonyms which more accurately portray the event the fact finder should perceive. In addition to the word "tired," other words such as exhausted, fatigued, worn out, weary, rundown, drained, listless, dull, tuckered out, and pooped could be used.

E. SEEKING AGREEMENT WITH WITNESSES

2.24 Be Compassionate

Witnesses ordinarily deserve courteous treatment. Some witnesses may deserve righteous indignation, others may be verbally "attacked," but no one deserves to be questioned in an obnoxious manner. The cross-examiner can usually be much more effective by being politely assertive and persistent and by showing appropriate compassion rather than aggression.

Example

Q: Ms. Lindberg, I understand this is a difficult time for you. We all know the kidnapping and death of your son was a terrible tragedy. You understand that I need to ask you some questions about the event so all of us understand what happened?

2.25 Enhance the Self-Interest of the Witness

An effective way to obtain a responsive answer to a leading question is to ask a question which makes the witness look good. Witnesses are much more likely to agree with a position that serves their self-interest or enhances them in some way. For example, if the purpose is to get the witness to admit to being tired, then questions ought to be asked which show the witness had legitimate reasons to be tired.

Sample Dialogue

Q: Tom Sawyer, you consider yourself a good worker?

A: Yes.

Q: You work hard when your job requires it?

A: Yes.

Q: Part of your work is demanding?

A: Yes.

Q: You want to succeed at your job, don't you?

A: I'd like to, yes.

Q: You try to do the best possible job you can?

A: I try.

These and additional questions lead to the inevitable conclusion that a hard working and dedicated employee who worked a full day would naturally be tired at the end of that day. Positive, supportive, and flattering questions usually result in an agreeable witness.

2.26 Establish Concepts With Witness

One of the purposes of cross-examination is to provide the fact finder with a different perspective and explanation of a situation. These perspectives and explanations can be established on cross-examination by asking questions that develop these "concepts." The cross-examiner wants the witness to show agreement with a "concept" by agreeing with the question. A witness may balk at certain words used to establish the concept, however. The cross-examiner should then focus on establishing the concept and not necessarily force the witness to agree to specific terms.

Sample Dialogue

Q: You were exhausted at the end of the game, Mr. Thorpe?

A: No, I was not exhausted.

Q: You must have been tired?

A: Yes, I was tired.

2.27 Employ Indirection

Cross-examiners sometimes use indirection in asking questions. With indirect questions the witness does not perceive why a question is being asked or the purpose of a line of questioning until the point is made. During witness preparation, the direct examiner will advise the witness of the anticipated areas of cross-examination, and the witness may have some understanding of the purpose behind some questions. This advance information may not be sufficient to alert witnesses to all areas of cross-examination, and their nervousness and unfamiliarity with the legal process may reduce their ability to think clearly and anticipate questions, making indirection an effective tactic.

Sample Dialogue (Cross-Examining the Employee)

Assume the cross-examiner represents an employer who fired an employee who then sues the employer for breach of the employment contract. The employer in defense claims the employee was an "at will" employee and could be fired at any time without cause, and cross-examines the employee.

Q: You could quit your job at any time, Ms. Vanilla, is that correct?

A: Yes.

Q: The dwarfs could not force you to stay?

A: Not if I wanted to leave.

Q: Yes. If you no longer wanted to work there, you could leave?

A: That's true.

F. CONTROLLING RESPONSES

2.28 Know the Answers

A rule of cross-examination is to ask only those questions to which the answer is already known or reasonably anticipated by the cross-examiner. Surprises in cross are not fun. The answer may be known because it appears in a witness statement, a deposition, a document, or is within the knowledge of another person. If the witness refuses to answer the question properly, the source of the information can be used to impeach the witness. Additionally, because the witness knows that a source of information exists, the witness will tend to answer the question to avoid impeachment. In this way, the witness' response can be controlled.

Sample Dialogue

Q: You were driving your motorbike approximately 5 light-years an hour, isn't that correct Mr. Skywalker?

A: I'm not sure how fast I was going.

Q: You were going approximately 5 light-years an hour?

A: I don't know.

Q: You recall that you gave a written statement in this case to an investigator, correct?

A: Yes, I did.

Q: In that statement you said you were going approximately 5 light-years an hour?

A: Oh, that's right.

2.29 Avoid the Prejudicial Unknown

A cross-examiner might be tempted to ask risky questions to which the answers are unknown. It is usually a mistake for the cross-examiner to give in to the temptation and ask questions which are likely to yield evidence prejudicial to the cross-examiner. In these situations, the cross-examiner may be able effectively to impeach the witness by omission.

2.30 Listen and Observe

It is axiomatic that the cross-examiner should listen to the answers and observe how the witness responds. But there are many things going on during cross-examination to distract the cross-examiner. The cross-examiner must remember to concentrate on the task at hand, including listening to the exact answers and observing the subtleties and nuances of the responses. The advocate must remain alert in order to follow up on nonresponsive answers, to repeat or rephrase questions if a witness is perplexed, to make certain answers are clear and understandable, or to comment on the appearance and credibility of witnesses during summation.

Example

Q: You were not at the studio, were you, Ms. Davis?

A: No.

Does the answer "No" mean "No, I wasn't there," or "No, I was there"? The inflection the witness uses in responding may make the response clear. If not, the cross-examiner should follow up:

Q: That means you were not there?

A: That's right.

Example

Q: It is true that you don't remember what Mr. Hale said, right?

A: Yes.

This question is awkwardly phrased because it contains the words "true," "right," and the negative: "don't." The cross-examiner needs to clarify the response:

Q: Your answer is that you don't remember?

A: Yes.

Example

Q: Ms. Alice, you paid the restaurant bill?

A: . . . I think so.

Q: Excuse me, your facial expression indicated that you may not have understood that question.

2.31 Control the Witness

The most effective way to control witnesses is to ask questions to which they must agree. Fact questions that are accurate will require the witness to agree. Questions that contain an answer that the witness has previously provided will also prompt the correct response. Examples in the previous sections illustrate this type of control. Lengthy or imprecise questions or questions that contain conclusions may give the witness reason to hesitate in responding. Control can be retained by rephrasing inappropriate questions.

Avoid asking:

Q: At the time the fight started you were standing behind the bar at the cash register giving change to a customer, isn't that correct, Mr. Gleason?

A: Not really. I was watching to see who started the fight, and I saw your client hit the plaintiff.

Rather ask:

Q: A fight broke out, didn't it Mr. Gleason?

A: Yes.

Q: You were behind the bar?

A: Yes.

Q: You were standing at the cash register?

A: Yes.

Q: You were giving change to a customer?

A: Yes.

Additional ways to maintain control include:

Sample Dialogue

Q: You were standing behind the bar?
A: Well, yes, but I was looking up.
Q: You were standing behind the bar?
A: Yes.

2.31.1 Insisting on an Answer

Sample Dialogue

Q: You were giving change to a customer?
A: I heard this noise.
Q: My question was—you were giving change to a customer?
A: Yes.

2.31.2 Rephrasing the Question

Sample Dialogue

Q: You were giving change to a customer?
A: I heard this noise.
Q: Perhaps my question was not clear enough. Let me ask it again this way. When you heard a noise, you were handing change to a customer?
A: Yes.

2.31.3 Advising the Witness to Answer

Sample Dialogue

Q: You closed the cash register drawer?
A: As I was looking over in the corner.
Q: You walked away from the cash register?
A: A customer called me over.
Q: Mr. Gleason, please limit your answer to the question I asked in order to help the jurors understand what happened?
A: All right.

Q: You did walk away from the cash register?

A: Yes I did.

Q: After you closed the drawer?

A: Yes.

2.31.4 Further Advising the Witness

Sample Dialogue

Q: The customer asked you for a drink?

A: She was thirsty.

Q: She asked you for a bottled beer?

A: We do not sell beer on tap.

Q: Mr. Gleason, in the interests of time and clarity, please answer the specific question asked. If you do not understand the question, tell me and I will rephrase it so that it is clear.

2.31.5 Seeking Cooperation from the Witness

Sample Dialogue

Q: Mr. Gleason, during your direct examination you answered the questions that your attorney asked you. You will be able to give me that same degree of cooperation you gave your attorney, won't you?

A: I'll try.

2.31.6 Requesting a Curative Instruction

If a witness gives a nonresponsive answer, the judge can be asked to instruct the jury to disregard the answer that was not responsive to the question asked.

Sample Dialogue

Q: You walked down to the far end of the bar?

A: But I'm sure your client started that fight.

Cross Examiner:

Your Honor, we ask that you instruct the jury to disregard that last answer as being nonresponsive and improper.

2.31.7 Asking for Further Assistance

The judge or arbitrator may be asked to instruct the witness to answer the questions asked. Some may do this on their own to prevent a witness from being unresponsive. Others may refuse to assist the attorney and may tell the attorney to conduct the examination. It is ordinarily more effective to ask for assistance after a witness has failed or refused to directly answer a number of questions.

Sample Dialogue

Q: The bottled beer was in a refrigerator located below the bar, wasn't it?

A: I could clearly hear your client yelling.

Q: You bent down?

A: Just for a brief moment.

Q: You opened a refrigerator?

A: How else could I get the bottled beer out? It only makes sense . . .

Cross Examiner:

I object on the grounds of nonresponsiveness and ask that you instruct this witness to answer the specific question asked and try not to ramble on.

2.32 Close Loopholes

To increase the chances a witness will agree with a question, it may be necessary to ask a witness a series of preliminary foundational questions which prompt responsive answers.

Sample Dialogue

Q: You gave the police a description of the person you saw start the fight, correct?

A: Yes.

Q: The events were fresh in your memory?

A: Yes.

Q: The description you gave was accurate?

A: Yes.

Q: You wanted to assist the police in finding this person?

A: You bet.

Q: You did not withhold any information from the police about the description of this person?

A: I did not.

Q: You gave them the best possible description you could of that person?

A: Yes.

These preliminary questions lay a foundation requiring the witness to respond because no reasonable person would disagree with the resulting conclusion.

2.33 Avoid Asking One Question Too Many

Questions should be designed to produce necessary information. When that information is obtained, the attorney should stop asking questions. Asking too many questions may hurt the case because the witness is given another opportunity to explain an answer. Often, a point can be made in closing argument without having the witness answer a question regarding that point.

Sample Dialogue

Q: After the fight, you gave a description of the person who started the fight to the police?

A: Yes, I did.

Q: You told the police that person was about 5′8″?

A: Yes.

Q: Had brown eyes?

A: Yes.

Q: Black hair?

A: Yes.

Q: Was of medium build?

A: Yes.

Q: Now that description fits many people who live in this community, doesn't it, Mr. Gleason?

A: I will never forget the face of your client who started that fight.

The last question is an example of one question too many. The attorney can make that point in closing argument without having the witness agree with the conclusion.

2.34 Avoid Explanations

Questions that permit a narrative response, or that ask "how" or "why," invite disaster in a cross-examination. A witness should not be given an opportunity to explain something that diminishes the point made on cross-examination. The opposing attorney may ask questions on redirect examination, but the cross-examiner should not ask questions that prompt explanatory responses.

Sample Dialogue

Q: So tell us why you say my client Jack the Ripper did it?

A: I've never seen anybody commit such a brutal act. I'll never forget your client's face as long as I live.

G. EMPHASIZING POINTS

2.35 Expand Points

It may be more effective in making a point during cross-examination to ask a few questions instead of just one question on a topic. These additional questions may emphasize the point and may prevent the fact finder from missing a point because they missed the one question asked on that point.

Avoid asking:

Q: You had three drinks at the bar that evening?

Rather ask:

Q: You arrived at the bar at approximately 6 p.m.?

A: Yes.

Q: You ordered one martini?

A: Yes.

Q: And you drank that martini?

A: Yes.

Q: You ordered a second martini?

A: Yes.

Q: You drank the second martini?

A: Yes.

Q: Then you had a glass of wine?

A: Yes.

Q: You say you left the bar at approximately 7 p.m.?

A: Approximately.

Q: You had two martinis and one glass of wine during the one hour you were at the bar, Ms. Temperance?

A: Yes.

2.36 Save Point for Summation

It is obviously helpful to an effective cross-examination that the fact finder remember and understand the point made during cross-examination. Therefore, questions should be designed so that at the end of a series of questions the fact finder understands the point being made. Sometimes, it is necessary or more effective to ask questions with points that may not be obvious or clear. The reasons for asking these questions can be fully explained in final argument.

Sample Dialogue

Q: Officer Krumpkie, you consider yourself a good police officer?

A: Yes.

Q: You take pride in your work?
A: Yes.
Q: You have been a police officer for ten years?
A: Yes.
Q: You graduated from the Police Academy?
A: Yes.
Q: You regularly attend police training programs?
A: Yes.
Q: You hope someday to become a captain?
A: That would be nice.
Q: You were the detective in charge of the investigation in this case?
A: Yes.
Q: You spent many hours conducting that investigation?
A: Yes.
Q: You spent several weeks involved in that investigation?
A: Yes.
Q: You developed a profile of the person who you believe committed this crime?
A: Yes.
Q: It is fair to say that you had a feeling about the person who committed this crime?
A: That's just good police work.
Q: After further investigation, you selected three individuals who you thought may have committed this crime?
A: We initially narrowed our investigation to three individuals.
Q: Yes. And you further investigated this first person on your list of suspects?
A: Yes.
Q: You later decided that this first person did not commit the crime?
A: That's right.
Q: You then investigated the second person on your list?
A: We decided to continue our investigation.

Q: And after still further investigation, you decided the second person could not have committed the crime?

A: Yes, that's correct.

Q: You then shifted the investigation to this third person on your list?

A: Well, the investigation continued.

Q: And after still further investigation you eliminated this person as a suspect?

A: Yes.

Q: And then you began an investigation of Mr. West, the defendant in this case?

A: Yes.

During summation the advocate can argue how uncertain the police were regarding their suspicions about the defendant, how long a period of time it took to conduct their unsuccessful investigations, and how reluctant the police may have been to re-investigate the case if they had not arrested the defendant.

H. ASKING SAFE QUESTIONS

2.37 Repeat Supportive Direct Examination

The general rule is that direct examination testimony should not be repeated because the repetition of the direct will only emphasize the opponent's case. However, repetition of direct examination testimony will be effective if that part of the direct is supportive of the cross-examiner's case. Leading questions usually are the most effective way of presenting supportive evidence. Open ended questions may be effective only if the response is helpful, witness control is not a problem, and the answer will be short.

Sample Dialogue

Q: Humpty Dumpty, you approached the wall on your own?

A: Yes.

Q: You then decided to sit on top of the wall?

A: Yes.

Q: You were able to climb the wall on your own?

A: Yes.

Q: You sat on the top of the wall, correct?

A: Yes.

Q: Then you fell off the wall?

A: Yes.

Q: There was no one around when you fell off the wall?

A: That's right.

Q: And that was a great fall?

A: Sure.

Q: Some people came immediately to help you?

A: Yes.

Q: All the King's men came?

A: There were a lot of them.

Q: And all their horses?

A: Apparently.

2.38 Ask "Neutral" Cross-Examination Questions

With some witnesses it may not be necessary to cross-examine them after direct examination to obtain supportive information or to discredit them. Cross-examination, however, may be useful to spend some time with them so that the fact finder will not retain too favorable an impression of their testimony. With other witnesses problems may arise during cross-examination, possibly placing the cross-examiner in an awkward situation. The examiner may need some "safe" questions to get back on track. In these and other situations, the following cross-examination questions may be appropriate.

Sample Dialogue (Volunteer Witness)

Q: Mr. Bailey, you were asked to be a witness in this case by the attorney for the plaintiff, correct?

A: Yes.

Q: You were not served with a subpoena ordering you to come to court to testify, were you?

A: No.

Q: You are voluntarily testifying for the plaintiff?

A: I suppose so.

Sample Dialogue (Familiarity with Evidence)

Q: You have talked with the representative for the plaintiff about this case, correct Mr. Karamazov?

A: Yes.

Q: And you discussed the testimony that you were to give in this case?

A: Yes.

Q: You also previously talked to the plaintiff?

A: Yes.

Q: And you discussed with the plaintiff what happened in this incident?

A: Yes.

Q: And you talked with other witnesses in this case about this incident?

A: I may have.

Q: Before coming into court to testify today, you had some idea of what the plaintiff was going to say, didn't you?

A: Yes.

Q: And you also had some idea of what some of the other witnesses were going to say?

A: Yes.

Sample Dialogue (Reviewed Documents)

Q: You were not present in court when the plaintiff testified, were you, Ms. Anthony?

A: No.

Q: You had a chance to read the deposition of the plaintiff which was taken before this trial, didn't you?

A: I looked at it.

Q: And you had a chance to look at some written statements the attorney for the plaintiff showed you?

A: I did.

Q: And those statements contained the stories of some of the witnesses in this case?

A: I believe so.

Sample Dialogue (Favorable Testimony)

Q: You pretty much understood why the plaintiff had brought this lawsuit, Ms. Fierro?

A: Yes.

Q: You knew that your testimony would help the plaintiff's case?

A: I suppose so.

Q: In fact, you understood that the plaintiff expected you to testify favorably?

A: Well, I assume that's why they asked me to come.

Q: And your testimony is helpful to the plaintiff?

A: I suppose so.

Arguments may be made based on answers to the questions in summation that the witness appears biased, over-prepared by the other attorney, or has no real knowledge of the facts.

I. DESIGNING QUESTIONS FOR SPECIFIC WITNESSES

Certain witnesses require special consideration in both the formulation and delivery of questions. These witnesses include children, experienced witnesses, experts, and witnesses with communication problems. Simple words, a softer or more assertive approach, technical mastery, a different location for questioning, are some tactics that may be useful.

2.39 Cross-Examining the Evasive Witness

Some witnesses may give evasive answers to cross-examination questions even though the questions are phrased as effectively as possible. Some witnesses may display selective memory, forgetting information which hurts them and only remembering information which helps them. Rambling witnesses provide nonresponsive answers, defeating even the best efforts to control their responses. Occasionally, witnesses may take on an adversarial demeanor or hostile attitude, even though the cross-examiner is tactful and polite. Still other witnesses may repeatedly answer by saying "I am not sure," "I can't remember," or "Maybe," even though the question is simple and direct.

These evasive witnesses, if allowed to continue, usually destroy their own credibility. The fact finder will perceive these witnesses to be unreasonably evasive and disbelieve their story. One way to cross-examine them is to continue to ask them questions and permit them to continue to be evasive and unreasonable. The negative impact created by these evasive witnesses may extend beyond their story and adversely affect other parts of the opponent's case. Further, during summation, the cross-examiner can compare the selective memory of the witness during cross with their good memory on direct examination.

2.40 Cross-Examining Reputation Witnesses

Because the character of a party or witness is usually not an issue, few cases involve the examination of reputation witnesses. The credibility of each witness who testifies can be attacked by the testimony of another who states that the witness' reputation for telling the truth is poor. As a practical matter, this occurs infrequently because most people have good reputations for telling the truth. Also, it is difficult to locate a person who can convincingly testify to a witness' propensity for being untruthful. Consequently, the opportunities to cross-examine reputation witnesses do not arise often.

When such opportunities arise, reputation witnesses can be cross-examined like any other witness. They may also be cross-examined as to specific instances of misconduct which contradict the character trait in issue. Cross-examination questions can establish bad acts, prior misconduct, convictions, and other instances of misconduct which contradict the reputation established on direct examination. Some cross-examination techniques are:

If the reputation witness testifies that the witness has a good reputation in the community, the question, "Have you heard . . ." of specific instances of misconduct can be asked.

If the reputation witness testifies that in the witness' opinion the reputation of the character trait is good, the question, "Do you know . . ." of specific instances of misconduct can be asked.

Reputation witnesses can also be effectively cross-examined by questions which establish their lack of personal knowledge about the events of the lawsuit:

"You were not home when the fight occurred?"

"You did not see who started the fight?"

Another line of questioning may establish the limited knowledge of the reputation witness and the narrow basis of the testimony:

"Thousands of people live in the defendant's community? You have only talked to a few of them about the defendant's reputation for truth?"

or

"You only spend a limited amount of time with the defendant at work? You are unaware of how the defendant treats his family at home?"

Some jurisdictions restrict the type of questions that may be asked on the cross-examination of a reputation witness. All jurisdictions require that the cross-examiner have a good faith basis and available proof to establish the prior misconduct.

J. DISCREDITING CROSS–EXAMINATION APPROACHES

This part of this chapter describes and provides examples of cross-examination techniques which discredit evidence and impeach witnesses. Planning a discrediting cross-examination should include a review of these techniques and a determination regarding which of them should be employed. Some of these techniques overlap and may be combined when implemented.

Cross-examination can establish that the story told by a witness ought not to be believed because it is implausible, improbable, or impossible.

2.41 The Implausible Story

The story may be implausible because it does not comport with common sense or common life experiences. For example, a witness may testify that four years before the proceeding, while repairing floor tile in the hallway outside the office of the CEO of M & M Company, he recalled overhearing the CEO say these exact words: "I just placed an order for 750 units at a price of $138,000, F.O.B. Los Angeles, and they agreed to send a letter of credit before sending the bill of lading and to pay for transit loss insurance." The cross-examination of that witness may include repeating the highlights of the direct examination testimony to demonstrate the implausible nature of the story. The advocate may later argue in summation that the recollection of such detail is too implausible to be believed.

2.42 The Improbable Story

A witness' version of a story, or part of a story, may be improbable. It may be unlikely the story could have occurred the way the witness describes. For example, a witness may testify that she was no more than a hundred feet away from a building while peddling her bicycle at a speed of 15 miles per hour toward the building, when she saw the black smoke and heard the explosion. The cross-examination may consist of her repeating her direct examination testimony; and the cross-examiner may place a mark on a diagram showing her position in the alley at the time of the explosion. During summation, the advocate can use a mathematical formula for the number of feet per second a bicycle travels at 15 miles per hour to show that either she was at least 300 feet away or that she was peddling over 40 miles per hour, which, while possible, is unlikely.

2.43 The Impossible Story

Some witnesses may sincerely tell an impossible story. While they may honestly believe what they perceived and remember, they are still wrong. For example, a witness may testify that, while parked behind the crosswalk at the intersection of Oak and Elm, she saw the defendant's Monte Carlo traveling at a high rate of speed. The cross-examination may consist of the witness repeating the testimony. During the defendant's case, the cross-examiner may then call an investigator to introduce photographs taken through a car window from the spot where the witness said he was stopped showing a brick building blocking the witness' view.

2.44 Establishing Inconsistencies Between Witnesses

The story a witness tells may be inherently correct and complete, but contradict the story told by another adverse witness. Cross-examination can establish these inconsistencies. For example, Police Officer Hernandez testifies that Sergeant Schultz was holding the shotgun in her right hand with the barrel pointed toward the ground. The defense cross-examiner may have Officer Hernandez repeat part of this testimony to highlight it. Officer Giribaldi subsequently testifies for the defense that Sergeant Schultz held the shotgun in both hands with the barrel pointed at the deceased. The defense can then argue these material inconsistencies during summation and point out why a particular witness (Officer Giribaldi) ought to be believed. It is usually ineffective, and often argumentative, for the cross-examiner to question Officer Hernandez directly as to why his testimony contradicts the testimony of Officer Giribaldi.

Asking one witness to comment on the credibility of another witness or asking whether a witness believes another witness is also improper. Asking a witness if that witness agrees or disagrees with a story told by another witness is proper. For example, asking: "Do you believe Officer Hernandez is telling the truth?" is improper. However, in most jurisdictions, one may properly ask: "Officer Hernandez testified that Sergeant Schultz held the shotgun in her right hand. Do you disagree with his statement?"

2.45 Employing Impeachment Strategies

Impeachment is a tactic designed to reduce the credibility of the witness, the credibility of a story, or the credibility of another witness. Any witness may be impeached. Any declarant of a hearsay statement who does not appear as a witness may also be impeached. See Fed.R.Evid. 806.

2.46 Using Material Issues to Impeach

Effective impeachment covers material and significant issues. If an issue is collateral—immaterial or insignificant—the impeachment is usually ineffective or disallowed. Whether impeachment evidence is collateral depends upon its impact on the issues in the case and on the credibility of the witness. Impeachment evidence ought to be introduced if the evidence relates to an issue, reduces the credibility of a witness or is otherwise important.

Impeachment is most effective when it relates to significant facts or opinions adversely affecting the credibility of the witness or story. A "reasonableness" test is the standard that ought to be used to determine the value of impeachment material. If it is reasonable that the testimony of a witness might be affected by a certain factor, or if the witness' testimony is unreasonable because the witness has testified differently on separate occasions, then the impeachment is reasonable and should be conducted. The following examples illustrate the reasonableness factor:

If a witness is a good friend of a party, it is reasonable that the witness may be biased in favor of that party. If a witness is merely an acquaintance of a party, that fact may not reasonably establish bias.

In an attempt to establish bias on the part of the witness in favor of a party, a cross-examiner may succeed by showing that the witness is a current, satisfied employee of the party for whom the witness is testifying. On the other hand, it would be ineffective for the cross-examiner to attempt to establish bias if the witness had worked for the employer for one month ten years ago and had had no contact with the employer since that time.

Witnesses may reasonably be uncertain about an exact day of the week. For example, a witness may testify that the day of an event was a Tuesday when in fact it was a Wednesday. But, if a witness testifies at a deposition she was "pretty sure" it was the defendant who was driving the car, and then testifies at trial she "is certain" the defendant was driving a car, such a significant change in her opinion will make impeachment worthwhile.

A witness to a crime may testify that she was standing at a "book rack" when she saw the defendant. Investigation reveals the rack she stood by was a magazine rack and not a book rack. An attempt to impeach the credibility of the witness by showing the rack was for magazines and not books may be so insignificant that it is worthless.

Impeachment efforts regarding marginal issues usually backfire because the fact finder may conclude that if the marginal issue is the best defense the cross-examiner has, the defense must be very weak. Not many cases will involve an impeachment matter of such significance that the case will be won or lost because of such impeaching material. Cases involving highly significant impeachment material that destroys the credibility of a key witness usually will be settled or otherwise resolved before the proceeding. At the other extreme, many witnesses may have made prior statements that contain minor inaccuracies when compared with trial evidence. These inaccuracies may not be significant or worth the effort to impeach the witness.

2.47 Proving Impeachment Through Extrinsic Evidence

A witness may occasionally deny the impeaching evidence. For example, a witness may testify that he is not an employee of defendant corporation or a witness may deny having a felony criminal record. The cross-examiner is usually able to introduce extrinsic (meaning from a source other than the witness) evidence to establish the impeaching fact. For example, the cross-examiner may call the personnel director of defendant corporation to testify that the witness is an employee, or the cross-examiner may introduce a certified copy of the criminal conviction and ask the tribunal to take notice of that document.

Extrinsic evidence may not be admissible if the impeaching issue is collateral. An issue is collateral if there is no direct connection between the impeaching fact and the relevant issue in the case. For example, a witness may testify on direct examination that she saw a plate glass window crack as she was drinking her vanilla shake. The cross-examiner asks her whether, in fact, the shake was chocolate, not vanilla, and she denies that it was chocolate. The cross-examiner will not be able to call the fountain clerk to testify as to the flavor of the shake because the type of shake is only collateral and not related to any material issue. However, if the same witness testifies on direct examination that she saw the plate glass window crack when she was sitting in a booth, the cross-examiner may ask her whether she was in fact sitting at the soda fountain. If the witness denies sitting at the soda fountain, the cross-examiner may call the fountain clerk as a witness to testify that the witness was sitting at the soda fountain with her back to the plate glass window, preventing her from seeing out. This issue is non-collateral because it directly relates to the ability of the witness to see and perceive.

2.48 Responding to Impeachment Evidence

The cross-examiner must consider the tactics available to the direct examiner who must deal with impeachment. The direct examiner has a number of options when facing impeachment evidence.

First, the direct examiner can object to the attempted impeachment. The area of impeachment may be immaterial or insignificant and an improper topic for impeachment.

Second, the direct examiner may request that related statements be introduced immediately in an effort to reduce the impact of the impeachment. Jurisdictions commonly have a rule permitting the introduction of statements related to the area of impeachment contemporaneously with the introduction of the impeaching statement. See, e.g., Fed.R.Evid. 106. The rationale for this rule is to permit statements to be placed in proper and complete context. For example, a witness may testify during a deposition: "The car was traveling around 30 miles per hour. But it may have been going slower." On direct examination, the witness testifies that the car was traveling "around 20 miles an hour." On cross-examination, the cross-examiner introduces the prior statement that the car was traveling "around 30 miles per hour" to impeach the witness. The direct examiner can ask that the prior statement—"But it may have been going slower"—be introduced at the same time during cross-examination to present the complete context of the statement. This request should be granted, and the statement can be read from the deposition transcript to the fact finder by the direct or cross-examiner.

Third, the direct examiner can explain the impeaching evidence during the direct examination. It is less harmful if the witness voluntarily explains a mistake or problem on direct examination. For example, it is a preferred practice for a witness who made a prior inconsistent statement to admit and explain the mistake during direct examination.

Fourth, the direct examiner can have the witness explain the impeaching evidence during redirect examination. This may be necessary, even if the witness first explains it on direct examination, depending upon how damaging the information is and how it was elicited during cross-examination. For example, if a witness during direct examination testified there were three firefighters at the scene, and at cross-examination admits there were only two, a redirect examination question would be: "Why did you say there were only two firefighters at the scene during cross-examination?"

Fifth, the direct examiner may rehabilitate an impeached witness with a prior consistent statement, if it rebuts a charge of fabrication or improper motive or statement. See, e.g., Fed.R.Evid. 801(d)(1)(B). If there is a written prior consistent statement, the statement can be introduced as an exhibit. If the prior consistent statement was not written but made to another person, that individual may be called to testify to the prior consistent statement.

Sixth, in a jury trial, the direct examiner may request that the judge give the jury an instruction limiting the jury's consideration of the impeaching evidence to its effect on the credibility of the witness and not as substantive proof of the evidence.

K. AREAS FOR IMPEACHMENT

There are eight established areas of impeachment:

Interest, Bias or Prejudice
Competency Deficiencies
Inadequate Observation/Lack of Perception
Poor Recollection
Inconsistent Conduct
Prior Inconsistent Statements/Omissions
Criminal Records
Specific Instances of Untruthfulness

2.49 Interest, Bias or Prejudice

Witnesses may have an interest in a case that motivates them to testify in a certain way. This interest might be financial gain if the case is resolved favorably, or an emotional reason, such as pride or revenge, that can be satisfied through successful litigation. Establishing these factors on cross-examination can demonstrate the underlying motivation behind a witness' testimony and may substantially reduce the credibility of that witness' testimony.

Bias and prejudice are factors which prevent a witness from being impartial. A witness may have a bias in favor of, or a prejudice against, a party or a case. Bias or prejudice can result from a variety of causes. The basis for the bias or prejudice is usually a relationship the witness has with a party or an interest the witness has in the case. The most common causes stem from family or personal relationships, employment situations, and life experiences. Establishing these factors during cross-examination reveals the underlying influences which make impartiality difficult or impossible for a witness.

If a witness denies the existence of an interest or a relationship, extrinsic evidence of the fact can be established. The cross-examiner can introduce such a fact through a witness or a document authenticated by a witness.

Sample Dialogue (Prejudice)

Q: Mr. Bluto, you do not consider Popeye a friend, do you?
A: He is not a friend.
Q: You have argued with him over the years?
A: Yes.
Q: You have had many fights with him?
A: Yes.
Q: Popeye has taken Olive Oyl, the woman you love, away from you?
A: He's trying.
Q: That makes you angry?
A: Yes.
Q: It is fair to say, Mr. Bluto, that you hate Popeye?
A: Without a doubt.

Sample Dialogue (Bias and Interest)

In a personal injury case, the father of the plaintiff was a passenger in the car which the son was driving at the time of the accident. The father was not injured.

Q: You were the passenger in your son's car at the time of the accident. Correct Mr. McMurray?

A: Yes.

Q: Your son lived with you at that time?

A: Yes.

Q: And he lives with you today?

A: Yes.

Q: You have a close relationship with your son?

A: Yes.

Q: You talk to him about many things?

A: Yes.

Q: And you talked to him about this accident?

A: A few times.

Q: Your son has told you that he hopes to receive money in this case?

A: Yes.

Q: You and he were driving back to the university?

A: Yes.

Q: That is a private college?

A: Yes.

Q: Your son pays for part of his tuition at the college?

A: Yes.

Q: And you pay for the balance of the tuition?

A: Yes.

Q: And your son pays for all his expenses?

A: For most of them.

Q: The tuition and the expenses are quite high?

A: It is expensive.

2.50 Competency Deficiencies

The four competency requirements for a witness are: oath, perception, recollection, and communication. Cross-examination may establish that a competent witness has deficiencies which render testimony of the witness less credible. The competency requirements of perception and recollection are two areas most frequently attacked on cross-examination.

The two other requirements of oath and communication are not usually areas for cross-examination inquiry. If a witness is unable or has difficulty taking an oath or affirmation, the opposing attorney will argue that the witness is incompetent. After a determination is made that a witness has properly taken an oath or affirmation, that requirement will usually not be an effective area to be probed on cross-examination. Further, Federal Rule of Evidence 610, explicitly prohibits evidence of a witness' beliefs or opinions on religion to be introduced for the purpose of reducing or enhancing the credibility of that witness.

Occasionally, a child witness or another witness who has difficulty discerning the truth may be asked cross-examination questions to establish an inadequate or inappropriate understanding of the oath or affirmation. Because of the delicate nature of the issue and the vulnerable status of the witness, cross-examination on the matter of oath or affirmation may cause the fact finder to empathize with the witness and to perceive the cross-examiner negatively. Effectively cross-examining a witness on the abstract notions of truth is difficult. Cross-examination can be effective when a record exists showing the witness has lied under oath or affirmation previously, or has told a story different from that told on direct examination.

Communication problems that witnesses have will ordinarily not be effective areas for cross-examination. If a witness cannot communicate, an interpreter will translate the testimony in an understandable fashion. If a witness has difficulty communicating because of a disability, cross-examination inquiries may make the fact finder more sympathetic toward this vulnerable witness rendering the cross-examination ineffective. If a witness has difficulty because of nervousness or some other reason, that factor may be self-evident and may not require any cross-examination questions.

2.51 Inadequate Observation/Lack of Perception

To reduce credibility, the ability of a witness to observe an event or to perceive a situation may be challenged on cross-examination. Most witnesses do not observe or perceive everything, and the inadequacies of observations and the lack of perception may be established on cross-examination. Common causes for inadequate observation and lack of perception are:

The witness was not expecting the event.

The witness was distracted.

The event happened quickly.

The situation was unusual.

The event scared or surprised the witness.

The witness was doing something else during the event.

The witness' perception based on sight, taste, hearing, smell, or touch was influenced by other factors.

Specific details of the event or situation were not previously described by the witness.

If the witness denies the impeachment questions asked to establish a material fact, the cross-examiner can introduce extrinsic evidence of this fact through other evidence.

Sample Dialogue (Car Driver)

Q: Professor Corbiston, you were driving north on Elm?

A: Yes.

Q: You were on your way to school?
A: Yes.
Q: You approached the intersection of Elm and Oak around noon?
A: Yes.
Q: Your class begins at noon?
A: Yes.
Q: You were going to be late for that class?
A: Yes.
Q: You were anxious to get to school?
A: Yes.
Q: You were in a hurry?
A: A bit. But I wasn't speeding.
Q: You spend a fair amount of time preparing for classes?
A: As much as is necessary.
Q: You spend a fair amount of time thinking about your classes?
A: Yes.
Q: Sometimes you think about your classes when you're at home?
A: Yes.
Q: Sometimes you think about your classes when you are driving your car?
A: But I pay attention.
Q: You do think about your classes when you are driving?
A: Yes.
Q: Your class was on your mind as you drove north this day on Elm Street?
A: Yes, I suppose.
Q: As you approached the intersection of Elm and Oak, the stop and go traffic light turned red?
A: Yes.
Q: You stopped your car a few feet south of the intersection crosswalk?
A: Yes.
Q: You noticed there was a crossing guard standing on the sidewalk to your right?

A: Yes, she was on the southeast corner.
Q: You knew the crossing guard was there to help children cross the street?
A: Yes.
Q: While you were waiting at the intersection, you would from time to time glance up at the light to see if had changed?
A: Yes.
Q: And you looked around to see if there were any children in the intersection crossing the street?
A: Yes.
Q: I believe you said on direct examination you saw two children to your right talking to the crossing guard?
A: Yes.
Q: Your radio was on in your car at this time?
A: Yes.
Q: It was noon time and the news was on the radio?
A: It may have been.
Q: Cars were driving east and west through the intersection?
A: Yes, I saw some cars drive by.
Q: You saw them drive by?
A: Yes.
Q: You were not expecting to see an accident at that time, were you?
A: No.
Q: That surprised you?
A: Yes.
Q: It is fair to say when you first heard the collision you naturally got a little scared?
A: Yes.
Q: You had a passenger in your car that day?
A: Yes.
Q: You were driving to school with another professor, Professor Prosser?
A: Yes.

Sample Dialogue (Car Passenger)

Q: You were the passenger in the car with Professor Corbiston, correct?

A: Yes.

Q: You both were on your way to school?

A: Yes.

Q: During the drive you talked with Professor Corbiston?

A: Yes.

Q: He told you he was in a hurry because he was late for class?

A: Yes.

Q: He also told you that he was going to cover some new material in class that day and it was going to be difficult?

A: He said something like that.

Q: While the car was stopped at the intersection, Professor Corbiston made some remark about the crossing guard?

A: Yes.

Q: He said he wished he were a crossing guard instead of a law professor.

A: Yes.

Q: And you said "There is not much difference"?

A: Yes, as a joke, obviously.

Q: After the accident, both of you drove on to school?

A: Yes.

Q: You don't recall Professor Corbiston saying anything at all to you about the accident, do you?

A: No, I don't recall.

Q: You do recall that he said after the accident he was going to be late for class?

A: He said that.

2.52 Poor Recollection

Most witnesses will not remember everything they observed or perceived. Some witnesses might not actually recall what they say they observed or perceived. Other witnesses may have had their recollection influenced by what they learned after an event. Cross-examination can reveal reasons why the witness' memory is lacking or unduly influenced. Common factors that diminish the recollection of a witness include:

The passage of time.

The absence of any written record.

Discussing the matter with others.

Being involved in similar situations.

Inability to distinguish this event from others.

Matters that adversely affect the memory of the witness.

If the witness denies the underlying fact showing poor or absent memory, the cross-examiner can introduce a non-collateral fact through extrinsic evidence.

Sample Dialogue (Car Driver)

Q: After the accident, you immediately drove on to the law school?

A: Yes.

Q: You did not wait at the accident scene?

A: No.

Q: You did not give your name or address to anyone?

A: No.

Q: You did not tell anyone at that time what you saw?

A: No.

Q: While driving back to the law school, you discussed the accident with Professor Prosser, the passenger in your car?

A: Yes.

Q: You discussed what you saw?

A: We talked about it.

Q: As you were driving nearer to the law school, you began to think more about your classes?

A: Yes.

Q: You taught your two-hour class that day?

A: Yes.

Q: You stayed in your law school office and wrote some memos?

A: Yes.

Q: You did not talk about this accident with anyone else while you were at the law school?

A: No.

Q: After school, you went home for dinner?

A: Yes.

Q: You recall you told your family that you saw an accident that day?

A: Yes.

Q: You do not recall the details of what you told them, do you?

A: No.

Q: The day after the accident you again drove to the law school with Professor Prosser?

A: Yes.

Q: The two of you discussed the accident?

A: Yes.

Q: You talked about it for a few minutes?

A: Yes.

Q: One week later you talked to an investigator about this accident?

A: Yes.

Q: During that week after the accident you don't recall whether you talked to anyone else about the accident, do you?

A: No.

Q: Some time after you talked with the investigator you recall receiving an accident report form, don't you?

A: Yes.

Q: That was a blank form with instructions to be completed?

A: I believe so.

Q: You never filled out that form, did you?

A: No.

Q: You never made any written notes about the accident, did you?

A: No.

Sample Dialogue (Police Officer)

Q: Officer Glover, this event took place approximately two years ago?

A: Yes.

Q: You arrived shortly after the victim had been injured?

A: Yes.

Q: You immediately began an investigation, correct?

A: Yes.

Q: As part of that investigation you talked with witnesses at the scene?

A: Yes.

Q: During an average week would you say you talked to over a hundred different people?

A: It is difficult to say, but that's possible.

Q: You may talk to more than a hundred different people during your week?

A: Some weeks more, some weeks less.

Q: When you conduct an investigation and talk with a witness you complete a report, correct?

A: Yes.

Q: You cannot possibly remember all the details these witnesses tell you?

A: Not all.

Q: You also have investigated many accidents over these past two years?

A: Yes that's true.

Q: It is impossible to remember all the details that you yourself see?

A: Sure.

Q: That's why you need reports.

A: Yes.

Q: These reports need to be accurate?

A: Of course.

Q: And complete?

A: Yes.

Q: The reports need detailed information?

A: Yes.

Q: If the reports don't have the details, an accident can be confused with another?

A: Yes, that can happen.

Q: You complete a report to make a record of the investigation?

A: Yes.

Q: That written report refreshes your memory about the details of an investigation?

A: Yes.

Q: The investigation report you completed in this case included the important information the witnesses told you?

A: Yes.

Q: It also had all the important details that you saw?

A: Yes.

Q: There is no mention anywhere in your report that the streetlights were not working, correct?

A: There is no mention.

Sample Dialogue (Salesperson)

Plaintiff has sued defendant for breach of an express warranty made during a sale. The salesperson has testified under direct examination that he does not recall stating that the car had no major mechanical problems and denies that the plaintiff consumer asked whether the car had any major mechanical problems.

Q: You have been a salesperson with Courtesy Car Company for three years, Mr. Loman?

A: Yes.

Q: Would you say that you have sold three or four cars a week on the average over the three years?

A: That would be a fair average.

Q: You, of course, talked with each of these customers?

A: Of course.

Q: Some of these customers leave and come back to the car dealer a number of times before deciding to buy a car?

A: Yes.

Q: In addition to all these customers, you also talk with other potential customers who decide not to buy a car?

A: Yes.

Q: Would you say that you talk to another 20 or 30 potential customers during an average week?

A: That is more difficult to estimate. Some weeks more, some weeks fewer.

Q: With each one of these customers and potential customers you talk about the features of the cars they are interested in?

A: Yes.

Q: You talk about the exterior of cars?

A: Yes.

Q: You talk about the interior of cars?

A: Often.

Q: You talk about gas mileage?

A: Frequently.

Q: You talk about many features of the various cars the customers look at?

A: Yes.

Q: The plaintiff bought a used car from you two years ago?

A: Yes.

Q: When you first met her on the sales lot she was like any other customer to you, correct?

A: Yes.

Q: And when she returned to buy the car, she was also like any other customer?

A: Yes.

Q: Most customers ask you questions about the cars they are interested in?

A: Yes.

Q: And the plaintiff asked you some questions about the car she purchased?

A: I assume so.

Q: You cannot remember all the individual questions that all your individual customers ask you?

A: That's not possible.

2.53 Inconsistent Conduct

Testimony of a witness may be discredited because the conduct of the witness may be inconsistent with the witness' direct examination. If the witness denies the inconsistent behavior, the cross-examiner can introduce extrinsic evidence of non-collateral conduct. Cross-examination can disclose that the actions of the witness contradict the testimony.

Sample Dialogue

In a personal injury case, the plaintiff has testified regarding the extent of injuries to his lower back, including pain and suffering.

Q: Mr. Whipple, immediately after the accident you got out of your car?

A: Yes.

Q: You walked over to the defendant's car?

A: Yes.

Q: You then walked over to a gas station?

A: Yes.

Q: That was about a hundred yards from the accident scene?

A: I would guess so.

Q: You asked the gas station attendant to call the police?

A: Yes.

Q: You did not ask for an ambulance or for a doctor?

A: Not at that time.

Q: You then walked back to the accident scene?

A: Yes.
Q: You stood around and waited for the police?
A: Yes.
Q: The police arrived about fifteen minutes later?
A: Yes.
Q: You talked with the police?
A: Yes.
Q: You did not ask for an ambulance or a doctor at that time, did you?
A: No.
Q: A tow truck arrived?
A: Yes.
Q: You stood around and watched the tow truck tow your car away?
A: Yes.
Q: About an hour after the accident, the police drove you home?
A: Yes.
Q: You didn't ask to go to a hospital?
A: No.
Q: When you arrived home, you told your family about the accident?
A: Yes.
Q: You then ate dinner?
A: Yes.
Q: After dinner you and your wife went to a movie?
A: To relax.
Q: After the movie you went home and went to bed?
A: Yes.
Q: The next morning you got up?
A: Yes.
Q: You ate breakfast?
A: Yes.
Q: You went to work at the grocery store?
A: Yes.
Q: You did not go to see a doctor then?

A: No.
Q: You talked with some of your friends at work about the accident?
A: Yes.
Q: You worked a full day that day?
A: Yes.
Q: Later that day you decided to telephone your doctor?
A: Yes.
Q: You made an appointment to see your doctor three days later?
A: Yes.

2.54 Impeachment by Criminal Record

A witness may be impeached by introducing a prior criminal conviction of that witness. Federal Rule of Evidence 609 and similar state statutes determine the type of criminal convictions that may be used to impeach and the discretion the tribunal has to deny the admission of such impeachment evidence. In general, convictions for a crime of fraud, dishonesty, false statements, or felony convictions (generally convictions of crime punishable by a term in excess of one year) may be used if the conviction or the release from confinement occurred within ten years from the date of the present trial. Convictions may be inadmissable if their unfairly prejudicial impact substantially outweighs their probative value. The fact a witness has been arrested or convicted of misdemeanors or juvenile offenses is inadmissible as a basis for impeachment.

Most jurisdictions allow all witnesses to be impeached through cross-examination questions revealing criminal convictions, but some jurisdictions permit only party witnessses to be impeached by prior convictions. Questions may be asked of the witness that reveal the crime involved, type of conviction, date and location of the conviction, and the sentence imposed. Some jurisdictions do not allow cross-examination of criminal defendants in regard to prior convictions and only permit impeachment to be proven by the introduction of a certified record of the criminal conviction. To avoid unfair prejudice, cross-examination questions cannot usually delve into the facts or details of the crime. Ordinarily, direct or redirect examination questions may be asked of the witness to explain the circumstances of the conviction or crime to reduce the impact of the conviction and reduce the negative impact on the credibility of the witness. If the witness denies the conviction, the cross-examiner can introduce extrinsic evidence, commonly a certified copy of the judgment of conviction.

2.55 Impeachment by Specific Instances of Untruthfulness

Evidence relating to the untruthfulness of a witness may be introduced against that witness during the cross-examination of that witness. Federal Rule of Evidence 608(B) and similar state rules permit a witness to be cross-examined regarding specific instances of misconduct that relate to the untruthfulness of the witness. The cross-examiner may ask leading questions which show the witness has committed acts establishing an untruthful character.

Sample Dialogue

Q: You have lied in other situations in your life, haven't you?

A: I'm not sure what you mean.

Q: About three years ago, you applied for a job with Tamarac Industries, correct?

A: Yes.

Q: You filled out an application form for a job with Tamarac?

A: Yes, I did.

Q: On that application form, you wrote that you had five years experience as a sales manager, right?

A: Yes.

Q: You did not then have five years experience as a sales manager, did you?

A: Not necessarily as a sales manager.

Q: What you wrote on the Tamarac application form was untrue?

A: I didn't have that experience.

Q: That statement was a lie, was it not?

A: It was incorrect.

Q: Two years ago you applied for a job with Mission Bay Enterprises, correct?

A: Yes.

Q: You interviewed with the personnel director at Mission Bay Enterprises, correct?

A: I believe so.

Q: You told that personnel director you had previously worked for Tamarac?

A: I may have said that.

Q: Tamarac never hired you.

A: I never worked there.

Q: That statement you made to the Mission Bay personnel director was untrue?

A: Yes.

Q: That statement was a lie?

A: Yes.

These situations occur infrequently. The information needed to establish the untruthful character of a witness is seldom available. Even if the information is available, it may be inadmissable because it is unfairly prejudicial or collateral to the issues of the case. Further, the tactic may backfire, because the fact finder may perceive the attack to be unfair and unrelated to the issues they must decide.

Evidence of the untruthful character of the witness may be introduced through opinion and reputation by witnesses called to testify on direct examination. These witnesses may be cross-examined like any other witness, and they may also be asked questions about specific acts of truthfulness by the witness who is being impeached. Further, to contradict the testimony of these impeaching witnesses, other witnesses may testify on direct examination to the reputation for truthfulness of the witness who is being impeached. These witnesses may also be cross-examined like any other witness, and may be asked questions regarding specific instances of untruthfulness by the witness.

Sample Dialogue

A witness testifies on direct examination that a party has a reputation for truthfulness.

Q: Did you know the witness lied in the past to employers?

A: No, I didn't know that.

Q: Did you know he had lied to Tamarac when he falsely told them he had five years experience as a sales manager?

A: I was not aware of that.

Q: Did you know he lied to Mission Bay Enterprises when he told them he had worked for Tamarac?

A: No.

L. IMPEACHMENT STRATEGIES AND TACTICS

2.56 Prior Inconsistent Statements

The credibility of a witness may be diminished on cross-examination by the use of prior inconsistent statements. To be used on cross-examination, prior statements must be inconsistent or contradictory. The obvious point to be made is that the witness provided testimony on a previous occasion that was different from the direct examination testimony.

An alternative technique to impeachment is to use the prior statement to refresh the witness' recollection. This may occur when the witness is not fabricating information but has made a mistake or cannot remember a portion of an event. This can be accomplished by showing the prior statement to the witness.

There are situations when the cross-examiner wants to prove a fact and will prefer to refresh the witness' recollection rather than impeach the witness. If a witness on cross-examination forgets a fact the cross-examiner wants to establish affirmatively, it will be more effective for the cross-examiner to refresh the recollection of the witness through a prior written statement. The cross-examiner may use a leading question to introduce the answer, but displaying to the fact finder the source of the written prior statement may be more persuasive.

2.57 Impeachment Preparation

The cross-examiner has to be intimately familiar with the witness' prior statements so that prior inconsistent statements can be located easily during cross-examination. Impeachment through the use of prior inconsistent statements usually includes four stages:

Reaffirm direct examination testimony

Describe circumstances of prior inconsistent statement

Introduce prior inconsistent statement

Obtain witness response to inconsistent statement

2.58 Reaffirming Direct Examination Testimony

The cross-examiner commits the witness to the direct examination testimony by having the witness repeat the testimony to reaffirm the evidence. This ought to be done in a way that does not unnecessarily alert the witness to the cross-examiner's intentions. Direct examination testimony that differs from a prior inconsistent statement should be selected. Precise questions should be asked which restate as exactly as possible the direct examination testimony. The cross-examiner should avoid asking questions which paraphrase or improperly summarize the testimony to avoid disagreement from the witness. Repetition of the direct testimony will prevent the argument that there really was no inconsistency, will reduce the witness' ability to explain away some ambiguity in the direct examination testimony, and will highlight the contrasting answers for the fact finder.

2.59 Describing Circumstances

The cross-examiner can then lead the witness through a series of questions describing the circumstances and type of prior inconsistent statement. These questions establish the date, time, place, and circumstances of the previous statement. If the fact finder is to believe that the prior inconsistent statement is accurate, questions that establish the reliability of the prior statement ought to be asked.

Some prior inconsistent statements are admissible as substantive proof. Federal Rule of Evidence 801(d)(1)(A) provides that a prior inconsistent statement made under oath at a legal proceeding is not hearsay, but is substantive evidence. Some states provide that other prior inconsistent statements may also be considered substantive evidence. If the cross-examiner does not want the fact finder to believe that either statement is true, then questions that establish the reliability of the prior statement need not be asked.

The Federal Rules of Evidence and similar state rules no longer require the witness' attention be called to the circumstances of the prior inconsistent statement. However, strategic considerations usually mandate such an explanation. These questions explain the circumstances of the prior statement, increasing the fact finder's understanding of what happened and the impact of the inconsistent statements. These background questions also reduce the witness' opportunity to explain away the prior statement, further increase the anxiety felt by the witness, and highlight for the fact finder the importance of the witness' mistake. There is no required number of questions that should be asked to establish the circumstances. The case, the witness, the prior inconsistent statement, and the theory of cross-examination determine how many and which questions will be asked.

2.60 Introducing Statement

The cross-examiner then introduces the prior inconsistent statement. Usually, the most effective way is to read the inconsistent statement to the witness and have the witness admit making it. Another way to introduce the statement is to show the statement to the witness and have the witness read it. The problem with having a witness read a prior statement is that the witness may not read it with the same degree of emphasis as the cross-examiner. The opponent ought to be told of the source of the statement and either the page number or line number of the source. The prior inconsistent statement need not be marked, because it is not being offered as evidence. The reading of the prior written statement and the witness' affirmation of the answer is the evidence offered. See Fed.R.Evid. 615(a).

2.61 Obtaining the Witness' Response

Ordinarily a witness will admit to making the inconsistent statement. The direct examiner will most likely have instructed the witness to readily admit the statement. The direct examiner may even have covered it on direct examination, or plans to have the witness explain it away on redirect examination. Impeachment questions should not be asked on cross-examination which allow the witness an opportunity to explain away the inconsistency.

If the witness admits making the statement, the impeachment process is concluded. If the witness does not admit or recall making the prior inconsistent statement, the cross-examiner must prove that the statement was made. Usually, extrinsic evidence is introduced to prove the statement. The following sections describe the various types of prior inconsistent statements and the necessary extrinsic evidence.

It is highly unlikely that witnesses will deny they made a statement appearing in a transcript or that their signature does not appear on a written statement. A witness may attempt to be evasive and say the transcript may be inaccurate or the written statement is incomplete, but further questioning will usually be successful in having the witness admit the transcript or written statement is authentic.

Sample Dialogue

Q: You have told us you saw both cars just before the crash?
A: Yes that's true.
Q: Are you sure you saw both cars before the crash?
A: Absolutely!
Q: Do you remember when Investigator Lestrade visited with you the day after the accident?
A: Yes.
Q: That was at your home, wasn't it?
A: Yes.
Q: He asked you some questions, didn't he?
A: Yes.
Q: And he wrote your responses down in a statement?
A: Yes.
Q: Investigator Lestrade gave you a chance to read that statement, didn't he?
A: Yes he did.
Q: And you did read it?
A: Yes.
Q: You signed that statement, didn't you?

A: Yes.

Q: You signed it because it was true and correct?

A: Yes.

Q: You wouldn't have signed it if it wasn't true and correct, would you?

A: No.

Q: Now, in about the middle of that statement you told Investigator Lestrade: "I only saw the plaintiff's car before the crash."

A: If that is what it says.

This method of impeachment repeats the direct examination. An alternative method accomplishes the same thing but does not require that the direct examination be repeated. Repeating the direct examination may over-emphasize that information. The following alternative technique avoids highlighting the direct examination.

Sample Dialogue

Q: You only saw one car just before the accident, didn't you?

A: No.

Q: Are you sure you did not see just one car?

A: Yes I'm sure.

Q: Didn't you tell Investigator Lestrade you only saw one car?

A: I may have.

Q: Well, you do recall the day after the accident you told Investigator Lestrade you saw only one car?

A: I talked to an Investigator after the accident.

Q: And you gave him a statement?

A: Yes.

Q: He wrote it down?

A: Yes.

Q: You read it?

A: Yes.

Q: It was true?

A: Yes.
Q: You signed it?
A: Yes.
Q: Because you thought it was true then?
A: Yes.
Q: And in that statement you said, "I only saw the plaintiff's car before the crash."

2.62 Significant Prior Inconsistent Statements

The nature of the impeaching material may vary from significant to minor. Impeachment efforts should be made only with significant, material evidence. A witness may testify at a deposition that a car was a "light" blue color and at the trial state the car was "blue". It would usually be ineffective to attempt to impeach the witness based on this minor discrepancy, unless the precise color of the car was significant in the case. Minor inaccuracies will not adversely affect the credibility of the witness unless there is a pattern or a large number of them.

2.63 Introducing Contemporaneous Prior Statements

The direct examiner can request that additional portions of the prior statement be introduced contemporaneously with the impeaching part of the statement to prevent a cross-examiner from introducing selective facts out of context. Federal Rule of Evidence 106 and similar state rules permit an opponent to request that other relevant portions of the statement be read.

2.64 Types of Prior Inconsistent Statements

There are five major types of prior inconsistent statements:

Prior statements under oath.

Discovery responses and verified pleadings.

Written statements.

Oral statements.

Omissions.

The following sections demonstrate examples of each of these types and the extrinsic evidence that is necessary to prove impeachment if the witness denies the prior statement.

8.64.1 Prior Statements Under Oath

Prior statements under oath include testimony provided at depositions, administrative hearings, previous trials, motion hearings, preliminary hearings, grand jury hearings, inquests, and other proceedings.

Sample Dialogue

Q: Ms. Westby, you testified on direct examination that you were traveling in your car at 25 miles per hour just before you entered the intersection?

A: Yes.

Q: You further testified that you knew the speed to be 25 miles per hour because you had just looked at your speedometer immediately before driving through the intersection?

A: Yes.

Q: That is your testimony under oath today before this jury?

A: Yes, that is what I said.

Q: Do you recall that you previously testified under oath regarding the facts of this case?

A: Yes, I remember.

Q: You remember we call that procedure a deposition?

A: Yes.

Q: There was a court reporter there taking down your statements just like there is a court reporter here today?

A: Yes.

Q: You took an oath and promised to give truthful answers?

A: Yes.

Q: You recall that your attorney was there with you?

A: Yes.

Q: And you recall that I was there?

A: Yes.

Q: Before that deposition, you had an opportunity to talk with your attorney about the deposition?

A: Yes.

Q: You had an opportunity to prepare for the deposition and think about what happened at the intersection?

A: Yes.

Q: That deposition occurred just a few months after the accident?

A: Yes.

Q: The events of the accident were still fresh in your mind at the time of your deposition?

A: Yes.

Q: During your deposition, questions were asked of you and answers were given by you just like today in court?

A: Yes.

Q: At the beginning of the deposition you were advised that if you did not understand a question to say so and it would be rephrased.

A: Yes.

Q: The questions and answers at the deposition related to what happened at the intersection of May Avenue and Ridge Boulevard?

A: Yes.

Q: You answered those questions at the deposition as best you could, correct?

A: Yes.

Q: You gave complete and honest answers?

A: I tried.

Q: You did not withhold any information, did you?

A: No.

Q: Ms. Westby, I'm handing you a document. Please look at it. Is this a transcript of your deposition?

A: It appears to be.

Q: Please turn to page 63 and look at line 10. You were asked this question then: "How fast were you driving when you first entered the intersection?" Do you see that?

A: Yes.

Q: And your answer to that question was: "About 25 miles an hour. I'm not real sure." Do you see that?

A: Yes.

Q: The next question you were asked was "Did you look at your speedometer any time before you entered the intersection?" And your answer was "I don't believe so." Do you also see that response?

A: Yes.

Q: Those were your answers a year ago, under oath?

A: That's what is written here.

Q: And those are your answers?

A: Yes.

Q: Do you recall several months after the deposition going to your attorney's office to read your deposition transcript?

A: Yes, I recall that.

Q: And you read over the answers that you gave?

A: Yes.

Q: And you understood at that time that you could make any changes if you had said anything incorrect or untrue?

A: I believe so.

Q: After reading your deposition you signed the deposition?

A: Yes.

Q: Your signature appears on the last page of that transcript, correct?

A: Yes, that's my signature.

Q: Thank you, Ms. Westby. That concludes my questioning.

The redirect examination can include the direct examiner's introduction of any segment of the deposition that helps bolster the accuracy of the direct examination testimony, reduces the impact of the prior statement, explains what the witness meant to say during the deposition, or shows that cross-examining counsel attempted to use a response out of context.

Sample Dialogue (*continued*)

Judge:

Redirect, counsel?

Direct Examiner:

Q: Yes, your Honor. Ms. Westby, please turn to page 116 of that same deposition, and look at line 8. That question was asked of you later in the deposition and it reads "Do you have any other basis for determining how fast you were going just before you entered the intersection?" Do you recall that question being asked of you that day?

A: Yes.

Q: Would you please read to the jury from your deposition the answer that you gave that day?

A: I said, "My long years of driving experience. And it's likely, come to think of it, that I looked at my speedometer, which I often do."

Q: That was your testimony a year ago, under oath?

A: Yes.

Proof of Prior Testimony

If a witness denies giving a deposition answer, a statement appearing in a deposition may be proved by offering that portion of the original deposition transcript into evidence. In most jurisdictions, the original deposition is not part of the record and does not appear in the file. Usually, the advocate who took the deposition has possession of the original transcript. The certification page prepared by the court reporter is attached to the original transcript certifying it to be the original.

There are three ways to place a deposition transcript into evidence.

In some jurisdictions, **the judge** may take notice of the original transcript and receive it in evidence.

In other jurisdictions, **the advocate** must authenticate the document, overcome any hearsay problems, and establish the transcript as an original writing. The original transcript of the deposition, which contains an attestation by a notary public, is self-authenticating under the rules of evidence, and a copy is also self-authenticating. See Fed.R.Evid. 902(1) and 902(4). The transcript can be established to be an original writing or an admissible duplicate by the certification signed by the notary at the end of the transcript stating it is the original. See Fed.R.Evid. 1001(3) or 1001(4). Hearsay problems may be overcome in one of two ways. If the deponent is an adverse party, the transcript can be offered as a party admission. See Fed.R.Evid. 801. If the deponent is a non-party, the transcript may be offered solely for the limited purpose of impeaching the witness (not for the truth of the matter asserted) rendering the transcript non-hearsay. See Fed.R.Evid. 801(c). If the witness is a non-party and the transcript is offered as substantive proof in addition to its impeachment value, the transcript can be offered in evidence as a public record exception to the hearsay rule. See Fed.R.Evid. 803(a).

In a few jurisdictions, **the court reporter** may have to be called as a witness to establish that the reporter is a qualified reporter, that the reporter was present at the proceeding and swore in the witness, and that the reporter prepared a verbatim record of all questions and answers.

Prior testimony that appears in a judicial or other proceeding may be proved by introducing a certified copy of the transcript of that portion of the proceeding containing the witness' testimony. The clerk of court or other administrator can provide a certified copy of the transcript prepared by the court reporter. The transcript should usually be marked as an exhibit and introduced in evidence. The portion of the transcript that contains the prior inconsistent statement ought to be read to the fact finder.

2.64.2 Discovery Responses and Verified Pleadings

Prior inconsistent statements may appear in answers to interrogatories, responses to requests for admissions, a verified complaint, or other documents signed by the witness under oath.

Sample Dialogue

On direct examination, a party testifies that he cannot remember whether he received a memorandum. An answer to an interrogatory states he did receive the memorandum.

Q: Mr. Kreskin, you testified on direct examination that you did not receive the Houdini memorandum, is that correct?

A: Yes.

Q: You do recall that as part of this lawsuit, you received some written questions from us?

A: I think so.

Q: Those questions are called interrogatories?

A: Yes, I remember them.

Q: You, with the assistance of your attorney, provided us with written answers to those questions?

A: Yes.

Q: You swore under oath that the answers that you gave were true?

A: Yes.

Q: Do you recall question No. 5 which asked, "Identify all memoranda you received related to the Houdini file"?

A: That sounds familiar.

Q: Your sworn answer to that question in part was, "I recall receiving the Houdini memorandum."

A: If that is what it says.

Q: That is what you stated in writing under oath at that time?

A: Yes.

Q: You discussed your answers to those questions with your attorney?

A: Yes.

Q: You understood that you had to provide complete and accurate answers?

A: Yes.

Proof of Discovery Responses and Verified Pleadings

Discovery responses and verified pleadings that appear in the file can be proved by introducing those documents from the record. Discovery responses that are not in the file may be proved by introducing the originals of those documents, which are usually in the possession of the advocate receiving the response. The opposing attorney will usually agree that the originals are accurate and authentic, and the tribunal will receive them in evidence. The opponent will usually also agree that the original is accurate and authentic and that stipulation will be sufficient for the tribunal to receive the transcript into evidence.

2.64.3 Written Statements

Written statements include writings that have been signed, agreed to, or approved by a party. Writings include written statements given to a police officer or investigator, notes handwritten by the witness, typed statements that are signed by a witness, affidavits in court documents, memoranda prepared by the witness, letters, business records, and other documents.

Sample Dialogue

The witness has testified that the defendant was not present at a meeting on December 1. In a memorandum the witness prepared and signed, the witness stated the defendant was present at the meeting.

Q: Mr. Marple, you have told us that the defendant, Ms. Krinkell, was not present during that December 1 meeting, correct?

A: That's right.

Q: You remember the other two people who were there but not the defendant?

A: She was not there.

Q: After that meeting on December 1, you prepared a memorandum?

A: I may have.

Q: It was your normal business practice to prepare a memorandum after a meeting that summarized the meeting?

A: Yes, it was.

Q: And after the December 1 meeting, you prepared such a memorandum?

A: I am not certain.

Q: I hand you what has been marked for identification as Defendant's Exhibit No. 6. Your initials appear on this memo?

A: Yes.

Q: It is dated December 1?

A: Yes.

Q: It summarizes a meeting that occurred at 3 o'clock p.m. that day?

A: It appears to.

Q: That is the memorandum you prepared after the December 1 meeting?

A: Yes.

Q: In the first paragraph of that memo, you identified the individuals who were present at the meeting?

A: Yes.

Q: You state in that memo: "Present were Sam Wilkins, Sam Shepard, and Dorothy Krinkell."

A: Yes.

Q: In that memo you identified Ms. Krinkell as being present at that meeting?

A: It appears so.

Proof of Written or Signed Statements

If a witness denies making a prior written statement, the prior statement can be proved by calling any witness who can identify the writing or the signature of the witness. The questions are the same as those needed to authenticate a document.

2.64.4 Oral Statements

Any oral statement a witness has made to anyone may be used as a source for impeachment. This includes oral statements made to investigators, police officers, business personnel during a meeting, friends at a social gathering, or to any person at any time at any place.

Sample Dialogue

A witness to a robbery was interviewed by a police officer and told the officer that she did not see the person who robbed the bar. The prosecution called this witness and on direct examination she identified the defendant as the robber.

Q: On direct examination, you testified the defendant was the person in this saloon?

A: Yes.

Q: You identified the defendant as the person who robbed the saloon?

A: Yes.

Q: You believe it was the defendant who was in the saloon the day it was robbed?

A: Yes.

Q: Ms. Kitty, you do recall talking to Marshal Dillon shortly after the robbery?

A: Yes.

Q: Marshal Dillon asked you what you saw?

A: I think so.

Q: You wanted to help the Marshal find the robber?

A: Yes.

Q: You wanted to tell Marshal Dillon everything you knew?

A: Yes.

Q: Marshal Dillon was taking notes when he talked to you?

A: I'm not sure.

Q: Ms. Kitty, at that time you told Marshal Dillon that you did not see the person that robbed the saloon.

A: I don't recall saying that.

Q: Ms. Kitty, you told Marshal Dillon that you did not know who robbed the saloon.

A: I don't believe I said that.

Proof of Oral Statements

If the witness denies making the prior oral statement, the previous oral statement can be proved by calling any witness who can testify that the witness made the prior statement.

Sample Dialogue (*continued*)

Q: Marshal Dillon, did you speak to Ms. Kitty shortly after the robbery?

A: Yes.

Q: Did she say anything about the robbery?

A: Yes.

Q: What did she say?

A: She said she did not see the person who robbed the saloon.

Q: Anything else?

A: She also said she did not know who the robber was.

2.64.5 Omissions

A common method of impeachment involves the cross-examination of a witness regarding a matter testified to on direct examination that does not appear in a prior written statement. Witnesses frequently fail to include all important details in prior statements. The omission is significant because there is no record of this material statement in any report, statement or testimony. The absence of this important information can be revealed on cross-examination and be used to reduce the credibility of the witness.

The impeachment process by omission is similar to impeaching with a prior inconsistent statement except the omission does not appear in the prior statement. A witness who testifies to an important matter that does not appear in a prior written statement can be impeached by establishing the absence of this material matter from the previous statement. Common prior statements which may omit significant facts include reports by police officers, memoranda by investigators, deposition testimony, and testimony in other proceedings. The impeachment process can establish that the prior statement was made at a time when the events were fresher in the witness' mind and can suggest that the witness may be adding facts or making things up because the statements were not included in the prior statement. This process is a subtle form of impeachment because the cross-examiner is establishing the nonexistence of a fact or opinion.

Sample Dialogue

In an automobile accident case, the plaintiff, Mr. Hardy, has testified on direct examination that the defendant said, "I am sorry. It was my fault." In his previous deposition the plaintiff never testified the defendant said those words.

Q: On direct examination, you stated the defendant, Mr. Laurel, said to you after the accident, "I am sorry. It was my fault."

A: Yes, that's what he said.

Q: Your testimony is the defendant made that statement to you immediately after the accident?

A: Yes.

Q: Now, Mr. Hardy, you recall your deposition was taken in this case?

A: Yes.

Q: At that deposition you testified under oath just like you were testifying under oath today?

A: Yes.

Q: Your attorney was present at that deposition?

A: Yes.

Q: And I was there asking you questions about the accident?

A: Yes.

Q: You remember I told you if you did not understand a question I asked you should tell me and I would rephrase it so you understood it?

A: I believe so.

Q: That deposition was taken about six months after the accident?

A: Yes.

Q: And the accident happened over two years ago?

A: That's about right.

Q: Before that deposition you talked with your attorney about the accident?

A: Yes.

Q: And after that deposition you had an opportunity to read the transcript of what you said and make any changes on it?

A: Yes, I believe so.

Q: You recall that during the deposition I asked you this question—on page 35 line 16: "What did Mr. Laurel say to you immediately after the accident?"

A: I believe so.

Q: And you recall your answer: He said "I am sorry this all happened."

A: If that's what it says.

Q: I show you your deposition transcript and ask you to read the next question that was asked you on line 18.

A: "Did the defendant say anything else?"

Q: Please read line 19 with me as I read it out loud. It says "No, I don't believe so." Right?

A: Yes.

Q: Nowhere in these answers did you say the defendant said, "It's my fault."

A: That's correct.

Sample Dialogue

On direct examination, a police officer testified he found a note in the defendant's pocket with the victim's name and phone number on it. That statement does not appear in his written report.

Q: Inspector Tragg, after you arrested the defendant, you searched his pockets?

A: Yes.

Q: On direct examination, you said you found a note in one of his pockets?

A: Yes.

Q: You also told us the victim's name and a phone number were on that note?

A: Yes.

Q: You are sure about that?

A: Yes.

Q: After you arrest someone you prepare a written report?

A: Yes.

Q: You have been trained on how to prepare such a report?

A: Yes.

Q: You were trained to include all important facts?

A: Yes.

Q: You were trained to prepare a complete and accurate report?

A: Yes.

Q: After you arrested the defendant, you prepared such a written report?

A: Yes.

Q: You wanted the report to include all important matters?

A: Yes.

Q: And you wanted that report to be complete and accurate?

A: Yes.

Q: Let me show you your report. This is your written report, correct?

A: Yes.

Q: After you completed the report, you read it over?

A: Yes.

Q: You made the corrections in your own handwriting on the report, right?

A: Yes.

Q: And after reading and correcting it, you signed it?

A: Yes.

Q: One of the purposes of this report is that the prosecutor relies on it to determine what happened, true?

A: Yes.

Q: Another purpose is to help you refresh your memory before testifying at trial?

A: Yes.

Q: You read this report before testifying here today?

A: I looked it over.

Q: You looked it over to help you remember what you did that evening?

A: In part, yes.

Q: Inspector Tragg, nowhere in this report did you state that you found a written note on the defendant?

A: That's not in the report.

Q: Nowhere in this report did you state that you found a note in the defendant's pocket?

A: That's not in there.

Q: Nowhere in the report did you state that you found a note with a name and phone number written on it?

A: That's not in the report either.

Proof of Omissions

Once the witness admits the information is missing, the impeachment is completed and the omission has been proved. If the witness denies the omission, the relevant portion of the transcript or the written statement must be introduced and shown to the fact finder to prove the absence of the significant fact or opinion. Omissions can be proved by introducing the prior written statement using the same methods to introduce deposition transcripts and documents described in the previous subsections.

2.65 Concluding the Cross

The cross-examination should be concluded with a significant point supporting your case and with a question you are certain the witness will answer in your favor. If not, select a topic and question that will. You usually want to end the closing with an important, sure, and non-objectionable question. Maybe you may want to—and effectively can—ask a question you don't care or really want the witness to answer—just like in the movies. But, decide if you want to be a method actor or an effective advocate. If you can be both, be both. If not, be an advocate.

*

RESOURCES

Bibliography

The Art of Cross Examination: A Case Study, Fredric G. Levin, 9 *Trial Diplomacy J.* 33 (1988).

Cross Exam—Bias, Prejudice or Interest, William F. Conour, 27 *Res Gestae* 535 (1984).

Cross Examination, Robert R. Michael, 23 *The Maryland Bar J.* 19 (1990).

Cross Examination, A Conservative Viewpoint, William R. Wilson, Jr., 3 *Trial Diplomacy J.* 24 (1980).

Cross Examination—A Primer for Trial Advocates, Jeffrey H. Hartje, 8 *Amer. J. of Trial Ad.* 11–55 (1984).

Cross Examination: "The Art of Gentle Persuasion," Tom Riley, 6 *Trial Diplomacy J.* 22–26 (1983).

Cross Examination: The Greatest Legal Engine for the Discovery of Truth, Michael R. Black, 15 *Southern Univ. L. R.* 397-405 (1988).

Cross-examination, David Austern, 22 *Trial* 15 (1986).

Cross-examination, Scott Baldwin, 17 *Trial Lawyers Quarterly* 19–26 (1985).

Cross-examination, Robert U. Bokelman, 22 *Trial* 110 (1986).

Cross-examination, James W. McElhaney, 74 *ABA J.* 117 (1988).

Cross-examination, William A. Moorman and Jack L Rives, 27 *Air Force L. R.* 105–111 (1987).

Cross-examination, Paul Stritmatter, 22 *Trial* 92 (1986).

Cross-examination—The Old Rules are Still the Good Ones, Scott Baldwin, 23 *Trial* 76 (1987).

Cross-examination, Methods and Preparations, G. Fred Metos, 3 *Utah Bar J.* 11 (1990).

Cross-examining the Sympathetic Witness, Leonard M. Ring, 14 *Litigation* 25 (1987).

Cross-examining Witnesses: The Dos and Don'ts, Mark A. Dombroff, 23 *Trial* 74 (1987).

Cross-ups in Cross-examination (of witnesses), Susan Loggans, 15 *Trial Diplomacy J.* 177–182 (1992).

Crossing the Star (cross-examination) Scott Turow, 14 *Litigation* 40 (1987).

The Delicate Art of Cross-examination, Allan Browne, 5 *California Lawyer* 22 (1985).

Dirty Tricks of Cross-examination, Saul M. Kassin, Lorri N. Williams and Courtney L. Saunder, 14 *Law and Human Behavior* 373–384 (1990).

Don't Take the "Bait;" How to Avoid Cross-examination Traps, Roger J. Dodd and Larry S. Pozner, 29 *Trial* 120 (1993).

How to Piece Together the Rorschach Puzzle for Cross Examination, Philip S. Lieb, 9 *Family Advocate* 20 (1986).

Impeachment, Martha Stansell-Liming, 27 *Air Force L. R.* 161–170 (1987).

Leading and Impeaching the Hostile or Adverse Witness, Russell I. Marnell and Steven C. November, 207 *New York L. J.* 1 (1992).

A Letter in Which Cicero Lays Down the Ten Commandments of Cross-examination, Irving Younger, 61 *Law Institute J.* 804 (1987).

Observations on the Preparation and Conduct of Cross-examination, Marvin Womisky, 30 *The Practical Lawyer* 40 (1984).

The Perfect Question: Setting the Trap in Cross-examination, Paul Ivan Birzon, 78 *ABA J.* 78 (1992).

The Poisoned Pawn (cross examination), Aaron J. Broder, 200 *New York L. J.* 3 (1988).

Rules for Effective Cross-examination, Hyman Hillenbrand, 14 *Brief* 46–49 (1985).

The Runaway: Seven Ways to Interrupt a Witness During Cross-examination, James W. McElhaney, 74 *ABA J.* 109 (1988).

Some Cross-examination Tips, Rex Conrad, 15 *ALI–AA Course Materials J.* 59–68 (1990).

Some Things Every Lawyer Should Remember About Cross-examination, Jacob D. Fuchsberg, *Personal Injury Deskbook* 609–616 (1985).

The Story Line in Cross-examination, James W. McElhaney, 9 *Litigation* 45 (1982).

The Three Techniques of Cross-examination, Herbert J. Stern, 16 *Trial Diplomacy J.* 49–57 (1993).

Vital Elements in Preparing the Witness for Cross Examination, Henry B. Rothblatt, 18 *Trial* 48–51 (1982).

Witness Explanations During Cross-examination: A Rule of Evidence Examined, Jeffrey A. Boyll, 58 *Indiana L. J.* 361–374 (1982–1983).

Criminal Cases

Confrontation, Cross-examination and Discovery: A Bright Line Appears After Pennsylvania v. Ritchie, Chris Hutton, 33 *South Dakota L. R.* 437–467 (1988).

Criminal Procedure: Illegally Obtained Evidence Used to Impeach the Accused on Cross Examination, Blaise R. Plummer, 20 *Washburn L. J.* 443–452 (1988).

Cross Examination of Accomplices, William F. Conour, 30 *Res Gestae* 517 (1987).

Cross Examination of the Alibi Witness, Bill Cunningham, 16 *Prosecutor, Journal of the National District Attorneys Association* 30–31 (1981).

Entrapment—Use of a Prior Indictment to Prove Defendant's Predisposition, Douglas A. Giron, 15 *Suffolk University L. R.* 771–778 (1981).

How to Expose Perjury Through Cross Examination, Alan Saltzman, 95 *The Los Angeles Daily J.* 4 (1982).

Opportunity of Criminal Cross-examination to Impeach a Witness for Bias or Motive, Tracey McCusker, 19 *Suffolk University L. R.* 494 (1985).

Specific Cases/Witnesses

Controlling the Runaway Witness: Tried and True Techniques for Cross-examination, Larry D. Pozner and Roger J. Dodd, 27 *Trial* 110–114 (1991).

Cross-examination of the Child or Sex Victim, Peter N. Carey, 27 *Air Force L. R.* 125–131 (1987).

Discrediting a Witness on Cross-examination: Non-party Witness, Edward M. Ricci, *Personal Injury Deskbook* 617–629 (1985).

Opportunity for Cross-examination of Guardian Ad Litem Required in Child Custody Proceedings, Anthony Todd Brown, 37 *South Carolina L. R.* 119–123 (1985).

Video

The Basics of Cross-Examination, Trial Practice, Anderson Publishing (1990).

Comparative Cross Examination in a Criminal Case, National Institute For Trial Advocacy (1976–77).

Comparative Cross Examination of a Rape Victim in a Criminal Case, National Institute For Trial Advocacy (1976–77).

Cross Examining the Biased Witness, National Institute For Trial Advocacy (1987).

Cross Examining the Child Witness, National Institute For Trial Advocacy (1987).

Cross Examining the Expert Accountant Witness, National Institute For Trial Advocacy (1987).

Cross Examining the Expert Attorney Witness, National Institute For Trial Advocacy (1987).

Cross Examining the Expert Medical Witness, National Institute For Trial Advocacy (1987).

Cross Examining the Eyewitness, National Institute For Trial Advocacy (1987).

Cross Examining the Hostile Witness, National Institute For Trial Advocacy (1987).

Cross Examining the Law Enforcement Witness, National Institute For Trial Advocacy (1987).

Cross Examining the Sympathetic Witness, National Institute For Trial Advocacy (1987).

Cross Examining the Well-Prepared Witness, National Institute For Trial Advocacy (1987).

Cross Examining the Witness of the Opposite Sex, National Institute For Trial Advocacy (1987).

Direct and Cross Examination in a Civil Case, National Institute For Trial Advocacy (1979).

Direct and Cross Examination of the Defendant in a Criminal Case, National Institute For Trial Advocacy (1977).

Direct and Cross Examination of a Party in a Civil Case, National Institute For Trial Advocacy (1978).

Direct and Cross Examination of a Rape Victim in a Criminal Case, National Institute For Trial Advocacy (1976–1977).

Direct and Cross Examination of a Witness in a Criminal Case, National Institute For Trial Advocacy (1976–1977).

Direct and Three Comparative Cross Examinations of a Major Prosecution Witness in a Federal Narcotics Case, National Institute For Trial Advocacy (1976–1977).

Mastering the Art of Cross Examination, National Institute For Trial Advocacy (1987).

Film

Suspect (1987).

Jagged Edge (1985).

The Verdict (1982).

Kramer vs. Kramer (1979).

Oh, God (1977).

To Kill a Mockingbird (1962).

Inherit the Wind (1960).

Anatomy of a Murder (1959).

Witness for the Prosecution (1957).

Adam's Rib (1949).

Miracle on 34th Street (1947).

Cross-examination (1932).

CHAPTER 3
EXPERT EXAMINATION

The life of the law has not been logic; it has been experience.

— Oliver Wendell Holmes

A. EXPERTS

3.01 When to Use an Expert

An expert should be used when the scientific, technical, or other specialized knowledge of the expert will assist the fact finder in understanding the evidence or in determining a fact that is in issue. In both simple and complex cases, expert testimony may be needed in order for one or both parties to prove their case.

3.02 Purposes of Expert Testimony

Expert testimony serves one or more purposes:

An expert provides a fact finder with factual information. For example, a treating physician will testify to the injuries suffered by a civil plaintiff.

An expert may apply expert knowledge to the facts of a case and render an opinion. For example, a design engineer can explain information about product design and render an opinion regarding the defective design of a specific product.

An expert can explain scientific principles and theories. For example, in a homicide case, a forensic pathologist may explain the medical principles involved in determining the cause of death.

An expert can testify to test procedures and results. For example, a chemist can explain the testing procedures to identify cocaine and describe the test results which prove the substance to be cocaine.

An expert can explain real evidence introduced in the case. For example, a radiologist can explain x-rays to the jury.

An expert can interpret the facts and render an opinion regarding the likelihood of an event or occurrence. For example, an accident reconstruction expert may testify to the probability of causation in a civil case.

An expert can testify to the amount of recoverable damages in a civil case. For example, an economist can testify to the present value of projected lost earnings of an injured plaintiff.

An expert can render an opinion which contradicts the conclusions of an expert who testified for the opposing party. For example, a psychiatrist can testify that a defendant was not mentally ill at the time the crime was committed, which conclusion directly contradicts the expert opinion of a psychiatrist called by the defense.

3.03 Who is an Expert?

A person who has specialized knowledge gained by education, training, experience, or skill may be qualified as an expert. Many professionals who have had extensive formal education and training may be readily qualified, such as doctors, engineers, and economists. Other individuals whose expertise has been derived primarily from experience or skill may also be readily qualified if they have the requisite experience and skill, such as mechanics and technicians.

3.04 Areas of Expertise

An area of knowledge that contains scientific, technical, or other specialized information may constitute an admissible area of expertise. A general test that many jurisdictions apply is: whether the area of expertise has gained general acceptance within the relevant scientific, technical, or other specialized expert community. A scientific theory which has gained general acceptance within the relevant scientific community or which has been verified by reliable testing, has been published in credible journals, and has undergone peer review is ordinarily recognized as an admissible area of expertise. These fields of expertise include medicine, engineering, economics, psychiatry, accounting, and law. Additional fields of generally recognized expertise include firearm analysis, ballistics, mechanical repairs, laboratory analysis, and property assessments.

An area of expertise will ordinarily be recognized if experts in the area and related areas recognize and accept the area as one reflecting specialized knowledge. Areas that are not traditionally considered areas of expertise or that are unusual may not be recognized as an area of expertise. For example, individuals proficient in operating lie detector machines are not usually considered experts because their opinions and lie detectors have not been recognized as accurate or reliable.

Some fields of expertise are not widely accepted and many require proof of reliability. These fields include hypnosis and voice spectograms. An expert may need to be asked questions to establish this reliability: "How well recognized is this area of expertise? Do experts like yourself recognize this area as reliable and accurate?" "Do experts like yourself wish you were rather a lawyer and had a job that really benefits society?"

3.05 Preparation for Expert Testimony

The direct examiner should know the subject on which the expert will testify as well or better than the expert. Without this specialized information the attorney may miss critical information, present information that will subject the expert to devastating cross-examination, or will be unable to identify errors or discrepancies with the testimony of the opposition's experts. The direct examiner may hire consulting experts in the field to assist in this educational process. These experts need not be called to testify but only serve to educate the advocate and offer suggestions for the cross-examination of opposing experts.

B. DIRECT EXAMINATION OF EXPERT

3.06 Qualifying the Expert

The rules of evidence require that the expert must be qualified in the area about which the expert will testify. See Fed.R.Evid. 702. The judge or arbitrator rules on whether an individual is "competent" and qualified to be an expert witness. This determination includes whether:

The expert has the education, training or experience in a field that is beyond the general knowledge of the fact finder.

The expert has sufficient information on which to testify in the particular case.

The opinion is based on the education, training and experience of the expert as applied to the information and is not based on unfounded speculation or conjecture.

Examples demonstrating the legal foundation necessary for almost every area of expertise may be found in many articles and books on the subject of expert examinations. The following list illustrates common areas of qualifications.

- Name
  - Title, degree
- Personal Background
  - Address (work, home)
  - Family
  - Length of residence
  - Hobbies
  - Clubs
  - Social organizations
  - Charitable organizations

How, When Expert Becomes Involved
- Treating physician
- Consultant
- Examination for trial (plaintiff or defense)
- Neutral expert
- Retained by plaintiff or defense
- Fees

Occupation
- Employer
- Position/description/responsibilities—how long
- Prior employers/positions/responsibilities

Education
- Undergraduate degrees
  - Institution
  - Graduation date
- Advanced degrees
  - Institution
  - Graduation date

Training
- What
- Where
- When
- By whom
- Certificates/licenses

Professional Organizations
- Name
- Purpose
- Length of membership
- Authority in organization

Professional Achievements
- Books
- Articles
- Teaching
- Lectures
- Consultations with other professionals
- Awards/honors

Legal Experience
- As Witness
  - Plaintiff or defense
  - Frequency of testifying
- Consultant
  - Organization or parties
  - Frequency

- Specialized Experience
  - Type of experience
    - Tests
    - Examinations
    - Study
    - Consulting with others
    - Personal interview
  - Number of tests
  - Results
- Specific Examination or Tests Involved in Case
  - Why
  - When
  - Where
  - How
- Weaknesses
  - Weakness of profession
  - Weakness of expert
  - Weakness of opinion
  - Bias
  - Prejudice
  - Interest
  - Lack of information
  - Lack of testing
- Opinions
- Basis of Opinions
- Sources of Opinion
- Exhibits

After sufficient foundation has been laid to establish the qualifications of an expert, the direct examiner may continue with the questioning to elicit expert testimony. Some jurisdictions require that the direct examiner request that the witness be accepted as an expert or "tender" the witness as an expert before continuing with the testimony: "We tender Dr. Watson as an expert forensic scientist."

3.07 Establishing Qualifications

Qualifications may be presented in sequence at the beginning of the examination, or may be mixed throughout the examination and presented as they apply directly to a particular point. Whenever qualifications are established, an effort should be made to "humanize" the expert and show that the witness is also a good person as well as an expert. Some experts may appear arrogant when describing their background because in effect they are telling the fact finder how brilliant they are. The direct examiner should ask questions which personalize the expert, and the expert should answer in a modest, appropriate manner.

The following examples demonstrate two different ways of presenting an expert's qualifications.

(A) Qualifications at Beginning of Examination

Sample Dialogue

Q: The plaintiff calls Dr. Benjamin Casey.
Q: Dr. Casey, you are a medical doctor?
Q: Do you live in our city?
Q: How long have you lived in our city?
Q: Do you have family in the city?
Q: Where did you go to college?
Q: In what fields did you get your degree?
Q: Where did you go to medical school?
Q: When did you graduate from medical school?
Q: Did you continue your schooling after medical school?
Q: Where?
Q: Did you specialize?
Q: Explain what that means?
Q: Are you board certified?
Q: What does that mean?
Q: What experience do you have in your speciality?

Q: Have you done any lecturing or teaching in your specialty or related areas?

Q: Have you written any books or articles in the area or in related areas?

Q: Do you belong to any professional organizations?

Q: Have you ever testified in court before?

Q: How often?

Q: Have you testified for both the plaintiff and the defense?

It is more traditional, and usually easier, to present the qualification in sequence at the beginning of the examination. This approach may not be the most persuasive way of presenting the expert. Long qualifications presented in the abstract may tend to be boring as they do not directly relate to the case.

(B) Qualifications During the Examination

Sample Dialogue

Q: Dr. Casey, you are a medical doctor?

Q: Do you live in our city?

Q: How long have you lived in our city?

Q: Do you have family in the city?

Q: Where did you go to college?

Q: In what fields did you get your degree?

Q: Where did you go to medical school?

Q: When did you graduate from medical school?

Q: Did you continue your schooling after medical school?

Q: Where?

Q: Did you specialize?

Q: Explain what that means.

Q: Now Doctor, at my request, did you examine the knee of Mr. Baryshnikov?

Q: When was that?

Q: Where did the examination take place?

Q: How long did the examination last?

Q: Tell us what you did to perform the examination.

Q: While you were at medical school, did you have training in conducting this kind of examination?

Q: Have you had any specific training or education in injuries of the type that Mr. Baryshnikov has?

Q: Was that training and experience helpful to you in diagnosing his injury?

Q: How?

Q: Have you ever lectured on the type of injury that Mr. Baryshnikov has suffered?

Q: Have you written any books or articles in regard to that type of injury?

Q: Does your lecturing and writing assist you in diagnosing and treating injuries of this nature?

Q: How?

3.08 Alternative Approaches to Qualifications

Alternative ways to qualify an expert include submission of the expert's resume or stipulations to the qualifications of the expert. If the case involves many experts, complete or summary resumes of the experts may be submitted instead of questioning the experts about their qualifications.

Stipulations to the qualifications of an opponent's expert, may make it unnecessary for that expert to be qualified. A stipulation may be preferable to having the fact finder hear the qualifications of the other side's expert. This will be particularly true if the opponent's expert has better qualifications.

The direct examiner must consider whether the submission of resumes or an offer of stipulation is tactically wise. It may be more effective for the fact finder to hear the expert testify to qualifications. The offer of the opposing side to stipulate to qualifications may be refused, and qualifications may be established through testimony.

3.09 Expert Opinions

An expert will usually testify to a number of opinions. A case may involve a major and several subordinate or minor opinions. The attorney may need to use specific words as a predicate to the introduction of an opinion: "Do you have an opinion to a reasonable degree of certainty?:

Example

Q: Do you have an opinion based upon a reasonable degree of medical (or psychiatric, accounting, or other) certainty?

A: Yes.

Q: What is that opinion?

Example

Q: Ms. Osborne, based on your experience, training, and education in the area of fingerprint analysis and, in addition, based on your examination of the fingerprints that you found on the dashboard of the car and your comparison of those fingerprints with the known fingerprints of the defendant, do you have an opinion to a reasonable degree of certainty whether the fingerprints found on the dashboard of the car are the fingerprints of the defendant?

A: Yes, I do.

Q: What is the opinion?

A: The fingerprints that were found on the dashboard of the car identically match the defendant's left thumb and forefinger.

3.10 Outline of Expert Opinion

A summary outline of the direct examination of an expert ordinarily includes the following topics:

The subject matter of the opinion.

The theories or principles that support the area of expertise and opinion.

The sources of information relied upon by the expert.

Any standard tests or routine procedures used in the area.

Specific tests or procedures used in a case.

Other bases of the opinion of the expert.

The opinion or conclusion.

An explanation of the opinion and conclusion.

Most direct examinations of an expert follow the sequence of this outline. Each direct examination should be reviewed to determine whether a different sequence would be more effective.

3.11 Sources of Information

An expert witness should explain the sources of information or facts which support the opinion of the expert. Federal Rule of Evidence 705 and similar state rules permit an expert to give an opinion without first having to provide the sources of the information or facts underlying the opinion. This rule permits some flexibility in the order of the expert testimony. The expert may explain the sources either before or after rendering the opinion.

There are a variety of sources of information an expert may rely upon. These include:

Personal, firsthand information perceived prior to the proceeding.

Information obtained from other experts, documents, records, files, individuals, and other sources, prior to or at the proceeding.

Evidence including proceeding testimony heard by or told to the expert during the proceeding.

Hypothetical questions.

Whatever information the expert relies upon must be of a type "reasonably relied upon" by experts in the particular field in forming such an opinion. See Fed.R.Evid. 703. This broad standard permits an expert to testify to any source of information, whether it is admissible or inadmissible, as long as experts in the area reasonably rely upon such information.

3.11.1 Personal, Firsthand Information

An expert may have personal firsthand knowledge of information learned or perceived prior to the proceeding. The witness may testify to these sources after a proper foundation has been laid which includes the actual observations or perceptions made, when and where these observations occurred, how the expert made these observations and who was present, and a description of the observations.

Sample Dialogue

Q: Chief Morgan, were you at the scene of the fire?

A: Yes.

Q: When did you arrive at the scene?

A: We received the first alarm about ten minutes after the fire started, and I arrived about five minutes after we received the alarm.

Q: What did you see when you arrived at the casino building?

A: Flames were shooting out of all the windows on the west side of the building, and the walls on the east side had partially collapsed.

Q: What did you notice about the flames?

A: They were a very bright orange color and were spreading rapidly from north to south through the building.

Q: Who was at the scene of the fire when you arrived?

A: The owner of the casino.

Q: Did you talk with him?

A: Yes.

Q: What did he say?

A: He said, "It's all for the good. The carpeting was really dirty."

An expert who has firsthand knowledge about physical evidence may need to testify to establish the chain of custody of the exhibit. An expert who routinely handles and examines many physical objects may have no independent recollection of a specific exhibit. Notes made by the expert may be used to refresh a recollection of the expert. Questions may be asked which first establish the regular, standard or correct procedure always employed by the expert followed by questions which establish that those recognized procedures were followed with the specific exhibit.

3.11.2 Information Obtained From Other Sources

An expert may rely upon information from other than personal observations and experiences, as long as the type of information is relied upon by other experts in the same area to reach conclusions. This type of information may include evidence that is inadmissible at trial. The most common form of inadmissible evidence will be hearsay. For example, in practice an expert may rely upon a triple hearsay statement, which the rules of evidence would exclude as unreliable. If, however, experts ordinarily rely upon this source of information, this expert may rely upon this hearsay in forming an opinion.

It is unclear to what extent an expert can explain the inadmissible sources of information. Federal Rule of Evidence 703 permits an expert to describe the source of the information and to testify that the information was relied upon as the basis of the opinion; however, there is disagreement as to the admissibility of the actual information itself. The expert may be permitted to testify that the expert relied upon information from another person, but not what that person said or wrote if it is inadmissible evidence.

Sample Dialogue

Q: Doctor, have you ever examined the plaintiff?

A: I did not.

Q: Have you done anything in regard to the plaintiff?

A: Yes, I have.

Q: What have you done?

A: I have read the entire medical record of the plaintiff. I have spoken with Dr. Hayson, and I have read her medical reports. In addition, I have read the accident reports prepared by the police department and I have read the statements given to the police by the two witnesses to the accident.

Q: Doctor, what did Dr. Hayson say in her reports?

Opposing Counsel:

Objection, your Honor, inadmissible hearsay.

Judge:

Sustained.

Q: Is this the type of information that experts in the field of orthopedic surgery, like yourself, normally rely on to reach a conclusion or to form an opinion about a person's injuries?

A: Yes, it certainly is.

Q: Based upon this information, and your experience, training, and education, do you have an opinion about the nature or type of injuries suffered by the plaintiff?

A: Yes, I do.

Q: What is that opinion?

A: I cannot find any evidence the plaintiff has suffered any injury whatsoever.

3.11.3 Information Obtained at the Proceeding

An expert may base an opinion upon evidence introduced during the proceeding. The expert may learn of this information by sitting through the case, or may be provided this information by the direct examiner. The substance of this information must also be the type of information that an expert in the same area relies upon to form an opinion.

Sample Dialogue

Q: Dr. Jung, have you been here in court during the testimony of the defense psychiatrist, Dr. Freud?

A: Yes, the entire time.

Q: Have you been here during any other part of the trial?

A: No.

Q: Have you read any files or records concerning this trial?

A: Yes.

Q: What have you read?

A: I have read the court file of this case and the transcripts provided me by the court reporter at the end of each day of testimony.

Q: Is the type of information you received from listening to the defendant's psychiatrist and from reading the daily transcripts of the testimony of all the other witnesses, the kind of information a forensic psychiatrist generally uses to form an opinion as to whether the defendant knew what he was doing or whether he knew what he did was wrong at the time he shot the victim in the dream?

A: Yes, it is.

Q: Based upon this information and your education, training, and experience, do you have an opinion whether the defendant knew what he was doing or if he knew it was wrong at the time of the dream shooting?

A: Yes, I do.

Q: What is that opinion?

A: My opinion is that the defendant knew exactly what he was doing and he knew it was wrong when he did it.

3.11.4 Hypothetical Questions

An expert may base an opinion upon a hypothetical question. The direct examiner asks the witness the hypothetical question which contains facts that have been or will be introduced during the proceeding. The expert, not having personal knowledge of these facts and not having heard these facts, is asked to assume facts in forming an opinion. The Federal Rules of Evidence and similar state rules no longer require hypothetical questions to be used to introduce an opinion. They can be used, but are usually cumbersome and much less effective than relying on one of the previous sources of information experts can rely upon.

If used, hypothetical questions should be prepared in advance with the help of the expert. They should be written out in order to avoid mistakes and should be accurate, complete, and as short as possible. The direct examiner should practice reading the question so that the question can be presented in as interesting a way as possible. Long, complicated hypothetical questions usually serve little purpose as they become dull and very difficult to follow.

Sample Dialogue

Q: Dr. Hypocrates, I ask you for your opinion based on the following hypothetical facts: Assume that a thirty-nine year old citizen was employed as a groundskeeper in the Athens school system. He was riding a lawnmower to care for the grounds at Quigley Academy, which were hilly and wooded. This man was mowing at about a speed of two miles per hour. His hands were on the controls and he occasionally had to look back over his shoulder. The mower hit a stump that stuck out of the ground about eight inches high and twenty inches in diameter. The force of the impact knocked the man off the seat of the mower and he fell to the ground. He hit his head on the turf and became unconscious. A passerby saw the accident and came to his aid. When the man became conscious, after about five minutes, the passerby took him to Parthenon Hospital where he was examined. The examination included an x-ray of his head. The x-ray revealed a fracture line on his skull which extends from the anterior side of the external auditory meatus through the middle of the right parietal bone—about four inches. The man complains of severe headaches.

Doctor, assuming all these facts, do you have an opinion based on a reasonable degree of medical certainty whether this man's condition was caused by the fall and the injury to his head?

A: Yes.

The hypothetical question should not be used to argue the case. The more that is put in the question, the more there is a chance for exaggeration and error, and the more opportunities there are for the cross-examiner.

3.12 Narrative Questions and Responses

The direct examination of an expert witness parallels many of the approaches and techniques applicable to a lay witness. There are, however, some differences in strategies. A direct examiner usually wants an expert to answer narrative questions with explanatory responses. Many experts testify as if they were a teacher explaining information to the fact finder.

Experts will generally be permitted to testify with longer narrative responses. Some experts can provide useful suggestions regarding how their opinion ought to be introduced and what questions should be asked. A narrative answer should be monitored and interrupted if words or concepts need to be explained or if the expert is getting off the track or is boring.

3.13 Explaining Technical Terms

The direct examiner must understand and know how to pronounce all of the expert's technical terms. The testimony of an expert may necessarily include the use of technical terms because they are required to lay a foundation for an opinion or because they buttress the credibility of the expert. The direct examiner must make certain that technical terms the expert mentions are explained in plain language.

Sample Dialogue

Q: How does a stethoscope work?

Q: What is a CAT scan?

Q: You used the term "metacarpals." What are they?

Q: Mr. Washington, how does a surveyor do a triangulation?

The terms and their correct spelling are also important for the record. The court reporter and when necessary the fact finder should be provided with a list of the terms the expert will use along with their definitions.

Demonstrative exhibits and visual aids may be effectively used to help experts explain information. Charts, diagrams, models, and videotapes may be prepared which illustrate what an expert described.

3.14 Use of Treatises

Treatises include books, periodicals, and pamphlets. A treatise may be used on direct or cross-examination. The authenticity of a treatise may be established by a reliable authority, through the admission of a witness, through another verifying expert or through judicial, administrative, or arbitral notice. A treatise may be introduced as evidence for any purpose. Treatises do not become exhibits, but the portions of a treatise offered in evidence are read into the record.

When a treatise is in general use and is relied on in a particular field, most experts will admit that it is an authority. An expert cannot prevent being cross-examined by a treatise by saying the particular treatise is not recognized as an authority. If one witness is able to testify that the treatise is authoritative, it may be used to cross-examine another expert, even though that expert refuses to recognize the authority of the treatise. The authoritative parts of the treatise may be read by the attorney or by the expert. It is the verbal testimony that may be admitted for any and all purposes. Whether used for impeachment purposes or as substantive proof of its contents, a treatise may substitute for a live expert and may corroborate another expert's opinion.

Sample Dialogue

Q: Doctor, are you familiar with an article in the National Journal of Medical Research published in 1986, entitled "The Diagnosis of Migraine Headaches Suffered by Lawyers", by Dr. Langdell?

A: Yes, I am.

Q: Have you read that article?

A: Yes, I have.

Q: Have you used the information in that article in your work?

A: Yes, I have.

Q: Do you consider it authoritative?

A: It is a very reliable authority.

By the Examiner (*to Judge*):

If I may, I would like to read one sentence on page 4 of that article entitled, "The Diagnosis of Migraine Headaches Suffered by Lawyers."

Judge:

You may do so.

Examiner:

> "The severity of a migraine headache of an average lawyer bears a direct relationship to the number of clients who have not paid the lawyer for services rendered."

C. CROSS-EXAMINATION OF EXPERT

3.15 Preparing to Cross-Examine the Expert

Information about an expert must be obtained regarding the trial expert's identity, qualifications, opinions, basis for opinions, data and documents supporting opinions, information relied on in forming opinions, publications, and fees. To effectively cross-examine an expert, the advocate must become knowledgeable about the area of expertise involved in the case by studying the area, reading texts, and taking classes. The advocate's own expert in the case, colleagues, and other experts can be useful sources of needed information.

3.16 Cross-Examination Areas

The cross-examination approaches and techniques explained in this chapter that apply to lay witnesses also apply to expert witnesses. Additionally, this section explains other tactics that can be used to cross-examine experts. These approaches include both supportive and discrediting cross-examination:

- Supportive Cross-Examination
  - Obtain concessions
  - Criticize the other side's positions
- Discrediting Cross-Examination
  - Disclose expert fees and financial interests
  - Establish bias or prejudice
  - Attack sources of information
  - Show unreliable or insufficient information

Dispute facts
Show lack of thoroughness
Show insufficient testing
Establish existence of other causes
Show inappropriate or insufficient expertise
Establish differences of opinions among experts
Establish subjective opinions
Introduce inconsistent prior statements
Discredit hypothetical questions
Expose other deficiencies
Expose unreliability of expertise
Use treatises

Experts do not often change their opinion or admit making a major mistake on cross-examination. Thus, attacking the opinion of an expert is difficult. However, an expert's opinion can be indirectly attacked by establishing a few significant deficiencies.

The advocate must also "control" the responses of the expert witness. Some experts have testified many times, and may know as much or more about a specific subject than the advocate. The cross-examiner may therefore have difficulty controlling the responses from these experts by attempting to accomplish too much. The last part of this section presents questions that may be asked to reduce the risk of losing control of an expert while discrediting their testimony.

3.17 Obtaining Concessions

An opposing expert may be used to establish, agree with or corroborate positions and opinions propounded by supporting experts. Questions can be asked which obtain admissions regarding generally accepted theories, principles, and opinions among experts and which show that the opposing expert agrees with the cross-examiner's experts.

Sample Dialogue

Q: Do you agree with Dr. Jekyll that schizophrenia can be effectively treated with certain drugs?

A: Yes.

Q: One of those drugs is Schizophryn?

A: Yes.

Q: Another one of those drugs is Psychophryn?

A: In many situations.

Q: You heard Dr. Jekyll state that the conduct of the defendant on the day of the crime was a classic reaction of a person with a schizophrenic personality.

A: Yes, I recall that statement.

Q: You do agree with that conclusion?

A: I do.

This concession can be effectively used during summation. "The Prosecution's expert agreed with our expert. Mr. Hyde, who testified for the prosecution, testified in support of our position. He said . . . ."

3.18 Criticizing the Other Side's Position

The opposing expert may be used to criticize a part of the opposing party's position, statements or conduct. Questions can be asked which establish that what the opposing party said or did was not appropriate or was otherwise deficient.

Sample Dialogue

Q: After the butterfly valve failed to close completely, the defendant did not replace the valve, correct Mr. Papillon?

A: That is my understanding.

Q: Had the defendant replaced the butterfly valve at that time, this accident may not have happened?

A: That's true.

Q: After the accident, the butterfly valve marked as Plaintiff's Exhibit No. 2, was left outside exposed to the sun and the wind and other elements of the weather?

A: Yes.

Q: Those elements affected the condition of the valve as it sat outside for approximately a month?

A: Yes.

Q: If the defendant had placed the butterfly valve in a safe protected environment, say inside a building, the condition of the valve would have been protected?

A: Yes.

3.19 Expert Fees and Financial Interests

An expert usually receives money for time spent in preparing for and testifying. The amount of money may be revealed on cross-examination, inferring that the testimony is influenced by the fee. Sometimes the fee will be excessive. Further, financial interests in a case can be exposed if the expert has testified in similar cases, or for the opponent, or expects to testify in similar cases for the opponent in the future. These fees and interests infer that the expert may be influenced to testify favorably in order to receive future income.

Sample Dialogue

Q: Dr. Slackwell, you received a fee from the plaintiff's attorney for the hours you spent in preparing for this trial, correct?

A: Yes.

Q: And you received a fee for the hours you are spending in court during this trial?

A: Yes.

Q: You will be sending your bill for these fees to the attorney for the plaintiff?

A: Yes.

Q: The amount of those fees that you receive will be more than $6,400?

A: Yes.

Q: You have been asked to testify in previous cases by the plaintiff's attorney, correct?

A: Yes.

Q: And you testified in several similar previous cases?

A: Yes.

Q: And you expect to testify again in the future?

A: I may.

The direct examiner will often bring out the existence of the fee, the amount of the fee, and involvement in previous cases during direct examination to reduce the impact of this area of cross-examination. In addition, the direct examiner may ask redirect questions allowing the expert to explain that the opinion has not been influenced by the fees or any financial interest. This may not be an effective area for cross-examination if the cross-examiner expects to call an expert to testify on direct examination and that expert has similar fees and financial interests.

The cross-examiner should avoid the question, "You are being paid for your testimony today, aren't you?" An experienced expert witness will reply that the payment is not for the testimony but is compensation for time, and that the charges are the same fee for time whether the expert is in the office or is testifying.

3.20 Bias or Prejudice

A professional expert witness who testifies frequently may have developed an apparent bias or prejudice because of involvements in previous cases. There are a number of experts who only testify for one side because of circumstances (e.g., treating physicians who testify for injured plaintiffs), and there are experts who testify because of choice (e.g., insurance defense experts). Other experts may not testify exclusively for one type of party, but still may testify more often for one side.

The extent of the bias or prejudice is influenced by whether the expert has somehow been involved with the facts before liability arose or whether the expert was hired as an advisor to plan or support the case. If an expert was a treating expert or was retained before the case is filed, the expert can be shown to have been a major participant in the case. If an expert was retained after the case is filed, the expert will have been influenced by the fact that the expert knew what opinion the advocate wanted the expert to form and assert.

Sample Dialogue

Q: Doctor Mendoza, you have testified approximately twenty times in this type of case before?

A: Yes.

Q: Of those twenty times, eighteen have been on behalf of the defense?

A: I believe so.

Q: Approximately ninety percent of the times you have previously testified have been in support of the defense?

A: Yes.

The direct examiner may anticipate this line of questioning and portray the expert as an independent professional and not as a hired gun. The direct examiner may also conduct redirect examination to disclose any favorable aspects of the expert's involvement with the other side of such cases.

3.21 Inadequate Sources of Information

Questions may reveal that an expert relied upon incomplete or inadequate sources of information in forming an opinion. The inference is that the expert did not have all the available information necessary to form a proper opinion, or did not know of a source of information essential to forming an objective opinion. The expert may have received the information primarily from the attorney who hired the expert, the expert may not have had information disclosed by other experts in the case, or the expert may not have reviewed information essential to forming a proper opinion.

Sample Dialogue

Q: Doctor McIntyre, you based your opinion in this case on information that the plaintiff provided you, correct?

A: Yes.

Q: You were not present at the scene of the fire?

A: No.

Q: You never went to the scene of the fire, did you?

A: No.

Q: You never conducted your own investigation of the remains of the building?

A: I did not.

Q: You don't have any personal information about how the fire started?

A: No.

Q: You relied exclusively on the information the plaintiff provided you?

A: Yes.

Q: That information was contained in a written file?

A: Yes.

Q: You never talked to the owner of the building, who is the defendant in this case, did you?

A: No.

Q: You never talked to the fire marshal in this case?

A: No.

Q: You never talked to anyone except the plaintiff and members of the law firm representing the plaintiff, did you?

A: That's correct.

3.22 Unreliable or Insufficient Information

Some experts may base an opinion on subjective facts obtained from a party. This is particularly true of treating or examining physicians, psychiatrists, or psychologists who derive their information from a patient. The expert's reliance on this information suggests their opinion is unreliable because of the subjective, slanted nature of the information.

Sample Dialogue

Q: Doctor, you examined Ms. Bly's lower back, correct?

A: Yes.

Q: She told you she had some pain in her lower back, correct?

A: Yes.

Q: She told you she thought the injury she suffered in the boat accident caused that pain?

A: Yes.

Q: You relied on her regarding her claim of lower back pain?

A: Yes.

Q: You looked at her lower back that day?

A: Yes.

Q: There was no bruising in the area of her lower back?

A: No.

Q: There was no apparent muscle spasm present, was there?

A: No.

Q: You took no x-ray of her back?

A: No.

3.23 Disputed Facts

During direct examination the expert reveals the facts that form the basis for the expert opinion. Some of these facts may be in dispute. On cross-examination the advocate can ask the expert if the opinion would change if the expert relied upon other facts. If the expert agrees with this conclusion, the attorney can argue in summation that the opposing expert agrees with this favorable conclusion. If the expert disagrees with the conclusion, the advocate can argue that the opinion of the expert is suspect because the expert stays with the same opinion regardless of differences in facts.

Sample Dialogue

Q: Doctor Lavoisier, you based your opinion on the fact that the glucose content was five percent, correct?

A: Yes.

Q: If the glucose content were only four percent, would that fact affect your opinion?

A: It might.

Q: Would the fact that the glucose was less than three percent change your opinion?

A: Yes.

3.24 Lack of Thoroughness

Experts have limited amounts of time to spend in preparing and forming opinions. In many situations experts do not prepare all things carefully or thoughtfully. Questions can be asked which show how little an expert has done and how much more an expert could have done.

Sample Dialogue

Q: Doctor Rogers, you conducted a psychiatric examination of the defendant?

A: Yes.

Q: You met with the defendant for an hour and a half?

A: Yes, I interviewed him.

Q: The only time you spent with the defendant was those ninety minutes?

A: Yes.

Q: That is all the time you believed you needed to form an opinion?

A: It was a sufficient amount of time.

Q: If you had spent more time with the defendant you would have acquired more information?

A: Sure.

Q: That additional information may have affected the opinion that you formed about the defendant?

A: It's possible.

Q: You may have learned some things about the defendant you did not learn during your only interview with the defendant?

A: True.

Q: You could have given the defendant some tests?

A: There was no need to.

Q: You decided not to give any tests?

A: That's true.

Q: And those tests may also have given you more information about the defendant?

A: They may have.

3.25 Insufficient Testing

An expert may not have conducted sufficient tests or procedures to support an opinion. The cross-examiner's own expert can tell the examiner what tests an expert should have or could have conducted before being able to render an opinion. Questions on cross-examination can establish that the expert failed to conduct ordinarily necessary tests, did not obtain information that experts typically rely on before forming an opinion, and may not have obtained critical test results that would have changed the expert's opinion.

Sample Dialogue

Q: Doctor McCoy, you removed the cast two weeks after the break?

A: Yes.

Q: At that time, you did not test to determine any loss of weakness in the muscle, did you?

A: Not at that time.
Q: You did not believe it necessary?
A: No.
Q: And you did not conduct any test to determine any weakness with the nerve, did you?
A: No.
Q: You didn't think it was necessary?
A: No.
Q: You placed a new cast on?
A: Yes.
Q: You removed this cast four weeks later?
A: Yes.
Q: Some fractures require much more time in a cast, don't they, Doctor?
A: Yes.
Q: Serious fractures?
A: Usually.
Q: When you removed this final cast, you did not perform an electromyography, did you?
A: No.
Q: Isn't it true an electromyography, if performed early enough, would make it possible to demonstrate a weakness in a muscle or nerve before a permanent loss of strength developed?
A: In some cases, yes.

3.26 Existence of Other Causes

Often there are alternative explanations for expert opinions. Cross-examination can reveal those alternatives by establishing other causes in addition to the cause the expert bases the opinion on. The cross-examiner's expert can provide other possible causes of an event.

Sample Dialogue

Q: Doctor Zhivago, there can be other causes for back pain, can there not?

A: Yes.

Q: A degenerative condition can cause back pain?

A: Yes.

Q: Or stress?

A: Do you mean physical stress or mental stress?

Q: Physical stress.

A: Yes.

Q: And mental stress?

A: I suppose, yes.

Q: And infectious conditions?

A: Yes.

Q: Heredity?

A: Yes.

Q: Congenital conditions?

A: Yes.

Q: Even a preexisting injury?

A: Yes.

3.27 Inappropriate or Insufficient Expertise

The expertise of an expert may be in areas different from those directly involved in the case. An expert may have expertise in a very broad area, and the case may involve a very narrow area. Or an expert may have expertise in a very narrow area, and the case may involve a broader area of expertise. Some opposing experts may be vulnerable to these attacks based on the lack of education, training, experience, or skills in an area of expertise involved in the case.

The emphasis attached to this area of cross-examination depends upon how the opposing expert contrasts with the cross-examiner's own expert. If a broad area of expertise is applicable to the case, the cross-examiner should attempt to narrow the expertise of the opponent's expert. If a narrow area of expertise is appropriate to the case, the expert should attempt to broaden the expertise of the opponent's expert.

Sample Dialogue

Q: Ms. Wong, your Master's degree is in structural engineering?

A: Yes.

Q: You did not major in electrical engineering, did you?

A: I did not major in it, but I had some courses in it.

Q: Your experience has primarily been in the field of structural engineering?

A: Primarily.

Q: More of your professional life has involved the area of structural engineering as contrasted with the area of electrical engineering?

A: Yes.

Q: You have published numerous professional articles?

A: Yes, many.

Q: You have written articles on structural engineering?

A: Yes.

Q: You have written articles on bridge construction?

A: Yes.

Q: And you have written articles that have appeared in structural engineering magazines?

A: Yes.

Q: None of those articles deal with the electrical engineering issues in this case, do they?

A: Not directly.

Q: You have not relied on any of those articles as a basis for your opinion in this case, have you?

A: I did not need to.

Q: Because those articles did not deal with the matters at issue in this case?

A: They did not.

3.28 Differences of Opinion Among Experts

Opinions in some areas of expertise are subject to significant and legitimate differences of opinion among qualified experts. This is especially true in fields of expertise involving subjective or interpretive fields, such as psychiatry or economics. Questions can be asked which establish different experts have legitimate differences of opinion and the testifying expert has been sometimes wrong and sometimes right in the past.

Sample Dialogue

Q: Doctor Heller, it is difficult to predict with accuracy the rate of inflation for future years?

A: Yes.

Q: It is fair to say that prominent economists differ among themselves regarding the future rate of inflation?

A: Yes.

Q: This area of predicting the rate of inflation is subject to significant differences of opinion among experts?

A: Yes.

Q: You have been an expert economist for over twenty years?

A: Yes.

Q: During that span of time, you have had occasion to predict the rate of inflation?

A: Yes.

Q: Sometimes your predictions have been accurate?

A: Yes.

Q: And sometimes your predictions have been inaccurate?

A: Yes.

Q: You have disagreed with the predictions of experts whom you consider to be renowned in the field of economics?

A: Yes.

Q: And these experts who are authorities in their field and whom you recognize as authorities—have disagreed with your predictions regarding the rate of inflation in the past?

A: I suppose.

Q: And sometimes their predictions—and not yours—have been accurate?

A: Yes.

3.29 Subjective Opinions

An expert may admit that the opinion the expert reached is a matter of judgment and not based on some immutable principles. This technique is useful for areas of expertise that are more subjective in nature than scientific. For example, in areas of expertise that are based on interpretations, evaluations can effectively be attacked.

Sample Dialogue

Q: The assessment of the value of real property is not a science, is it Ms. Hubbard?

A: No, it is not a science.

Q: There are many variables that affect the value of a piece of property, correct?

A: Yes.

Q: Some of these variables are based on subjective evaluations and not objective data?

A: That is true.

Q: Some of these factors require an appraiser individually to interpret property values, correct?

A: Yes.

3.30 Inconsistent Prior Statements

An expert witness can be cross-examined using any oral or written statement by that expert that contradicts or is inconsistent with a position taken on direct examination, as with a lay witness.

Sample Dialogue

Q: Dr. Keynes, you testified on direct examination that the defendant properly used the FIFO method in this transaction because it is the "preferred method" employed by accountants, is that right?

A: Yes.

Q: Doctor, you prepared a written report summarizing your opinions of this case, didn't you?

A: Yes.

Q: The attorney for the plaintiff retained you and paid you for your time in preparing that report?

A: Yes.

Q: Before preparing the report you thoroughly reviewed all the facts, correct?

A: Yes.

Q: You consider yourself an expert with regard to accounting procedures, don't you?

A: Yes.

Q: The report that you prepared was accurate, wasn't it?

A: Yes.

Q: Doctor, I would like to show you your written report. You do recognize this report as the one you prepared, correct?

A: Yes.

Q: Your signature appears at the end of the report on page 5?

A: Yes.

Q: Please turn to page 3, second paragraph, 4th line.

A: Okay.

Q: You wrote what's contained on that line in that paragraph in that report, didn't you?

A: Yes.

Q: You wrote on line 4 that: "Neither the FIFO nor the LIFO method is preferred in a case such as this."

A: I see that.

3.31 Hypothetical Questions

If a hypothetical question is used on direct examination, an effective way to cross-examine the expert is to ask the expert concise hypothetical questions which contain facts different from the direct examination hypothetical. There are fewer opportunities to cross-examine the expert on the basis of the hypothetical facts because hypothetical questions are asked less often on direct examination.

3.32 Safely Exposing Deficiencies

Additional areas that can be established on cross-examination are topics that do not depend upon the facts and circumstances relating to the specific area of expertise. These areas include "safe" questions which can be asked if questions suggested in the previous subsections are not appropriate or are too risky:

The late entry of the expert into the case because the opposing advocate did not secure this expert until immediately before trial.

The very limited amount of time the expert spent reviewing the information and data.

The fact the information the expert relied upon has been provided primarily by the party who retained the expert.

The facts and information upon which the expert relied are not the facts upon which other testifying experts in the trial relied.

3.33 Lack of Reliability of the Field of Expertise

This area may be available if the direct examiner does not present an expert in the field of expertise presented by the opposing party's expert. The advocate should then attempt to ask cross-examination questions establishing the unreliability of the field of expertise and the failure of experts in that area to accept and recognize the area as a reliable field of expertise.

Topics that may be successfully covered using this approach include: the lack of education, experience, training, and skills the expert has; the differences between related areas of expertise that have been generally recognized and unrecognized; the unreliability of the procedures, tests, or opinions rendered; the observation that the field of expertise is nothing more than the application of common sense that the fact finder may apply.

3.34 Treatises

Treatises can be used during the cross-examination of an expert to impeach that expert as well as for other purposes. Federal Rule of Evidence 803(18) and similar state rules provide:

Treatises may be used on cross-examination of an opposing expert, just as they can be used on the direct examination of an expert.

Treatises include treatises, periodicals, pamphlets, articles, and professional magazines.

Treatises must be established as "reliable authority" by admission of a witness or by another expert or by notice.

Treatises may be introduced as evidence for any purpose.

Treatises are read into the record and do not become exhibits.

Some experts who have written extensively may have published a position contrary to their position taken at the proceeding. Other experts may be impeached by treatises another person authored. This impeachment process requires a thorough review of all the publications in the area and a detailed index of these publications.

An expert on cross-examination need only admit that a treatise is a reliable authority generally recognized in an area. The expert does not have to have relied upon the treatise or professionally agree to its position. Leading questions which establish that the treatise has successive editions, is used extensively in professional schools, or appears in the offices of many experts, may establish this foundation. If an expert on cross-examination denies the general reliability of the treatise, the treatise may still be used but will need to be established as authoritative by another expert, by notice, by the publisher of the book, or by a librarian. Some jurisdictions still require the witness on cross-examination concede that the treatise is authoritative and that the witness relies on it before it can be used for impeachment.

The cross-examiner offering the treatise may read it to the fact finder once the foundation for the treatise has been established. The treatise is admitted as evidence for all purposes: for impeachment, as substantive proof of its contents, to substitute for a live expert, or to corroborate another expert's opinion. The opinion of an author of a treatise or other learned publication can be introduced through the treatise even though the author does not testify.

Sample Dialogue

Q: Doctor, are you familiar with a text entitled, *The Economics of Law Practice*?

A: Yes.

Q: This text has been a reliable authority in the field of economics for many years, correct?

A: Yes.

Q: Do you consider this text to be authoritative?

A: It's one authority.

Q: Doctor, do you agree with the following statement that appears on page 169: "The increase of law firm income is in inverse proportion to the number of associates working less than 168 hours a week?"

A: In general, I agree.

To the Court:

Your Honor, I now would like to read a short paragraph from page 368 of the text.

Judge:

You may do so.

Examining Attorney:

"A major factor which law firm managers use to determine an associate's salary is based upon the formula equal to pi squared times the number of brief pages the associate has written."

No further questions.

D. COMPLEX CASES

3.35 Expert Testimony in Complex Cases

Complex cases seem to breed experts. Specialists with technical and other expert knowledge are needed to explain to the fact finders significant issues in a case. Experts should be used to provide information no available lay witness can provide. Complex cases also involve the use of informally retained and consulting experts who provide attorneys with essential information before a lawsuit ensues.

The problem with multiple experts in complex cases are that their opinions may be different and their opinions may be based on different reasons. It is important for both the opinions and the bases for the opinions to be as similar as possible to avoid apparent and real discrepancies.

Issues which need to addressed in complex cases include:

What type of expert is involved in the case? A trial expert? A retained expert? A specially employed expert? An employee expert? Or an expert who has both factual and expert knowledge?

Is the identity of the expert discoverable?

What is discoverable from this expert? Through interrogatories? By way of a deposition? Regarding documents?

How can this expert best assist the attorney in preparing the case?

How can an expert best assist the attorney during the trial of a case?

What are the qualifications of the expert?

What sources of information does the expert rely upon? Are these ordinarily relied upon by experts in the area?

Is all the information relied upon by an expert admissible? Need it be?

What are the opinions of the expert? Will the testimony of this expert be consistent with other experts in the case? How can the differences be reconciled?

What are the bases for the expert's opinion?

How will this expert be prepared? By whom?

How will this expert testify most effectively? Through narrative questions? Through specific questions? Through a mix of both types of questions?

What exhibits will be introduced through this expert?

What visual aids will be useful during this expert's testimony?

What writings has the expert authored that will be useful in the case? What materials may be adverse?

Are there any special areas of impeachment regarding this expert?

Will other experts in the case attack the credibility of this expert's opinion? How can this be best defended?

Why didn't I become an expensive expert instead of a lawyer?

RESOURCES

Direct Examination

Court-Appointed Experts, Thomas E. Wiliging (Federal Judicial Center 1986).

Direct Examination of Experts, Dennis R. Suplee and Margaret S. Woodrull, 33 *The Practical Lawyer* 53 (1987).

Direct Examination of Experts: How to Make Expert Witnesses Credible, David M. Malone, 24 *Trial* 42–49 (1988).

The Direct Examination of the Expert Witness, Joseph M. Costello, 28 *For the Defense* 21–24 (1981).

Direct Examination of Expert Witnesses (Master Advocate's Edition), Robert E. Ferencik, Jr., 27 *Air Force L. Rev.* 83–88 (1987).

Direct Examination of a Licensed Psychotherapist, George N. Statfield, 15 *Trial Lawyers Quarterly* 18–25 (1983).

Direct Examination of Medical Experts, Lawrence L. Longfelder and Kerry D. Kidman, 24 *Trial* 113 (1988).

Direct Examination of Plaintiff's Medical Expert—Emergency Room Malpractice Case, Arthur Ian Miltz, *Personal Injury Rev.* 807–819 (1990).

Direct Examination of a Treating Pediatric Neurologist in a Birth-Injury Case, Paul J. Giancola, 15 *Trial Lawyers Quarterly* 55–61 (1983).

Doctors and the Law: Defendant and Expert Witnesses, Miller B. Zobel and Stephen N. Rous (W.W. Norton & Co. 1993).

Expert Witnesses, Faust P. Rossi (Section of Litigation, American Bar Association 1991).

Expert Witnesses, Irving Younger (Professional Education Group 1984).

Expert Witnesses in Civil Trials: Effective Preparation and Presentation, Mark A. Dombroff (Lawyers Co-Operative Pub. Co./Bancroft-Whitney Co. 1987).

The Plaintiff: Choosing and Presenting Your Expert, Leonard M. Ring, 14 *Brief* 35–41 (1985).

Prepare and Present Your Expert Witness, Mark A. Dombroff, 26 *For the Defense* 15–23 (1984).

Presenting Expert Testimony, James H. Seckinger, 15 *Amer. J. of Trial Ad.* 215–268 (1991).

Qualifying Experts, James W. McElhaney, 11 *Litigation* 43 (1984).

Cross-Examination

The Cross Examination of Defendant's Doctor, A. Richard Barros, 8 *Delaware Lawyer* 18 (1990).

Cross-examination of the Defendant's Medical Expert, Thomas J. Vesper, 16 *Trial Diplomacy J.* 93–108 (1993).

Cross-examination of a Defendant in a Medical Malpractice Case, Alvin H. Broome, 20 *Trial Lawyers Quarterly* 42–51 (1990).

Cross-examination of an Expert, Lanny S. Vines, 18 *Trial Lawyers Quarterly* 41–48 (1987).

Cross Examination of Expert on Stock Values, R. Bertil Peterson, 16 *Trial Lawyers Quarterly* 53–61 (1984).

Cross-examination of an Expert Witness, R. Mark Halligan, 32 *For the Defense* 29–32 (1990).

Cross-examination of Experts, Alvin A. Wolff, Jr., 24 *Trial* 97 (1988).

Cross-examining the Defense Expert (Medical Negligence), Thomas A. Moor, 27 *Trial* 49 (1992).

Cross-examining the Expert at Trial (Trial Techniques: Tools of the Trade), Harvey Weitz, 28 *Trial* 55–58 (1992).

Defending Mental Injury Claims: Cross-examining the Plaintiff's Expert Witnesses, Eric H. Marcus, 11 *Trial Diplomacy J.* 37–42 (1988).

The Defense: Impeaching Your Opponent's Expert, Richard T. Jones, 14 *Brief* 42–45 (1985).

Expert Witnesses: Nine Ways to Cross-examine an Expert, James W. McElhaney, 75 *ABA J.* 98 (1989).

How to Cross-examine a Psychologist in a Custody Case, Thomas M. Mulroy, 7 *Amer. J. of Family L.* 65–72 (1993).

Successful Cross-examination of Technical Experts, Ted. M. Warshafsky, 15 *Trial Diplomacy J.* 89–94 (1992).

Taking on the Opposing Expert: An Approach to Cross-examination, David B. Baum, 20 *Trial* 74–78 (1984).

Using Surprise to Capture the Expert Witness, Scott M. Seaman and James F. Martin, 35 *For the Defense* 19 (1993).

Specific Cases/Witnesses

The Admissibility and Utility of Expert Legal Testimony in Patent Litigation, Howard G. Pollack, 32 *Idea* 361–381 (1992).

Admissibility of Expert Testimony on Child Sexual Abuse Accommodation Syndrome in Kentucky, Michele Meyer McCarthy, 81 *The Kentucky L. J.* 727–747 (1993).

Attacking Expert Testimony: How to Win the Battle of the Experts, Kurt L. Schmalz, 15 *Los Angeles Lawyer* 46 (1992).

Believe It or Not: How Much of an Expert Does an Expert Witness Have To Be?, Mark Hanse, 79 *ABA J.* 64 (1993).

Calling the Other Side's Expert, (in medical malpractice cases) (New York), Thomas A. Moore, 209 *New York L. J.* 3 (1993).

Choosing the Right Expert Witness, Joanne Ross Wilder, 12 *Family Advocate* 44 (1990).

Cross-examination of Expert Witnesses, Dennis R. Suplee and Margaret S. Woodruff, 34 *The Practical Lawyer* 41 (1988).

Cross-examining the Expert: Some Tips from the Bench, Hugh C. Humphreys, 23 *Trial* 75 (1987).

Direct and Cross of the Vocational Economic Expert, John Tierney and Valerie J. Ellien, 22 *Trial Lawyers Quarterly* 21–26 (1992).

Direct Examination and Cross-examination of Expert Witness (Transcript), Stephen I. Lane, Scott N. Lane, William J. Johnson, and Thomas J. Koch, 39 *Medical Trial Technique* 114–160 (1992).

An Effective Expert Witness, Eric H. Marcus, 31 *Trauma* 5–8 (1990).

Eliminating the Element of Surprise: Rethinking the Disclosure Requirements of Illinois Supreme Court Rule 220, Deanne Fortna, 17 *Southern Illinois University L. J.* 195–209 (1993).

Expert and Opinion Evidence in Vermont: Developments, Profiles, and Emerging Concerns for Reliability of Scientific Evidence, Kenneth R. Kreiling, 17 *Vermont L. R.* 109–164 (1992).

The Expert in a Product Case; Preparation and Cross Examination, Robert E. Cartwright and Jerry J. Phillips, 22 *Trial* 22 (1986).

Expert Testimony By Psychologists: Novel Scientific Evidence, Ernest S. Graham and Robert E. Kabacy, 14 *Law and Psychology R.* 71–85 (1990).

Expert Testimony in Title 42, 1983 Actions, Martin A. Schwartz, 208 *New York L. J.* 3 (1992).

Expert Testimony in Securities Fraud Cases, Edward Brodsky, 205 *New York L. J.* 3 (1992).

Expert Testimony on Decision Processes in Employment Cases, Donald J. Schwartz and Jane Goodman, 16 *Law and Human Behavior* 337–355 (1992).

Expert Witness Testimony: A Litigation Issue for Discharge and Discrimination Cases, Robert M. Vercruysse and James S. Rosenfeld, 72 *Michigan Bar J.* 146 (1993).

Fighting Back: Defense Use of Experts, (Criminal Law), Juanita R. Brooks, 29 *Trial* 42 (1993).

Getting Straight Answers from Experts, Amy Neustein, 25 *Judges J.* 30 (1986).

In Search of the Right Experts in Products Cases, Raymond P. Johnson, 28 *Trial* 36–41 (1992).

Is the Trial Deposition of an Expert Really Just an Interview? (Pennsylvania), John T. Hinton, 29 *Duquesne L. R.* 313–324 (1991).

Legal Perspectives: You Can Lose a Court Case Without Expert Testimony, Arthur Kornblut, 172 *Architectural Record* 43 (1984).

Limiting the Number of Expert Witnesses Under Rule 26(b)(4)(D): An Analysis of the Meaning of the New Rule, Bruce C. Smith, 25 *Arizona State L. J.* 167–194 (1993).

Living with Experts—20 Pungent Proverbs and 18 Little Gambits (Trial Strategy), Henry G. Miller, 192 *New York L. J.* 1 (1984).

Nature of Jury Response to the Expert Witness, Paul Rosenthal, 28 *J. of Forensic Sciences* 528–531 (1983).

Preparing the Difficult Medical Causation Case and the Cross Examination of Physicians from Medical Texts, Russ. M. Herman, *Personal Injury R.* 781–795 (1990).

Rule 703: Bases of Opinion Testimony By Experts, Charles J. Kall, 21 *Colorado Lawyer* 691 (1992).

The Rules and the Expert Witness, Michael J. Hoover, 49 *Bench & Bar of Minnesota* 11 (1992).

When Seeing is Not Believing, the Case for Eyewitness Expert Testimony, Cindy J. O'Hagan, 81 *Georgetown L. J.* 742–772 (1993).

The Winning Approach: Protect Yourself from Your Experts, Mitchell A. Cohn, 15 *Trial Diplomacy J.* 309–313 (1992).

Video

Comparative Cross Examination of an Economist Expert Witness, National Institute For Trial Advocacy (1977–1980).

Direct Cross Examination of an Expert Witness, National Institute For Trial Advocacy (1977–1980).

Direct Cross Examination of an Expert Witness: Pathologist, National Institute For Trial Advocacy (1977–1980).

Direct Cross Examination of an Expert Witness: Psychiatrist, National Institute For Trial Advocacy (1977–1980).

Direct Cross Examination of an Medical Records Custodian, National Institute For Trial Advocacy (1977–1980).

Direct Examination of an Expert Economist in a Civil Death Case, National Institute For Trial Advocacy (1977–1980).

Discovery of Expert Witnesses Under the Federal Rules of Civil Procedure, National Institute For Trial Advocacy (1988).

Effective Use of Expert Testimony in Closing Arguments, National Institute For Trial Advocacy (1988).

Examination of an Expert Witness, National Institute For Trial Advocacy (1979).

Examining the Economist, National Institute For Trial Advocacy (1988).

Examining the Hospital Administrator, National Institute For Trial Advocacy (1988).

Examining the Medical Doctor, National Institute For Trial Advocacy (1988).

Examining the Materials Engineer, National Institute For Trial Advocacy (1988).

Expert Witnesses: An Overview, National Institute For Trial Advocacy (1988).

Expert Witnesses, Cross Examination, and Impeachment I, National Institute For Trial Advocacy (1975).

Expert Witnesses II, Cross Examination II, and Rehabilitation I, National Institute For Trial Advocacy (1975).

Experts I Lecture, National Institute For Trial Advocacy (1977–1980).

Experts II Lecture, National Institute For Trial Advocacy (1977–1980).

Introducing Experts in Opening Statements, National Institute For Trial Advocacy (1988).

Persuasive Expert Testimony, National Institute For Trial Advocacy (1990).

Qualifying the Expert, National Institute For Trial Advocacy (1988).

Testimony of Expert Witnesses Under the Federal Rules of Evidence, National Institute For Trial Advocacy (1988).

Film

A Few Good Men (1992).

Eight Men Out (1988).

Rampage (1992).

Nuts (1987).

Verdict (1982).

The Caine Mutiny (1954).

The Secret Life of Walter Mitty (1947).

*

INDEX